Collins

HANDY ROAD ATLAS
SCOTLAND

KEY TO MAP PAGES

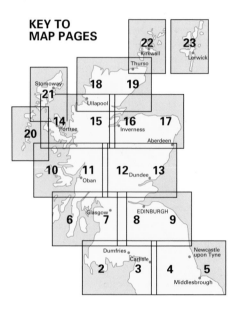

CONTENTS

Road Maps at 9 miles to 1 inch	2-23
Urban Area Maps at 4 miles to 1 inch	24-25
Aberdeen, Dundee,	24
Edinburgh, Glasgow	25
Index to place names	**26-30**
Street maps of city centres	**31-72**
Key to street map pages	31
Aberdeen	32-35
Index to Aberdeen	36-37
Dundee	38-39
Index to Dundee	40-41
Edinburgh	42-51
Index to Edinburgh	52-57
Glasgow	58-65
Index to Glasgow	66-72
Radio Stations	

Published by Collins
An imprint of HarperCollins*Publishers*
77-85 Fulham Palace Road, Hammersmith, London W6 8JB

The HarperCollins website address is: www.**fire**and**water**.com

Copyright © HarperCollins*Publishers* Ltd 2002
Mapping © Bartholomew Ltd 1997, 1998, 1999, 2000, 2002

Collins® is a registered trademark of HarperCollins*Publishers* Limited
Mapping generated from Bartholomew digital databases

Bartholomew website address is: www.bartholomewmaps.com

e-mail: roadcheck@harpercollins.co.uk

Pages 32-35, 42-51 and 58-65 are based upon the Ordnance Survey Mapping with the permission of The Controller of Her Majesty's Stationery Office © Crown copyright 399302.

Printed in Hong Kong   ISBN 0 00 448986 1   Imp 004   PC11294   CDU

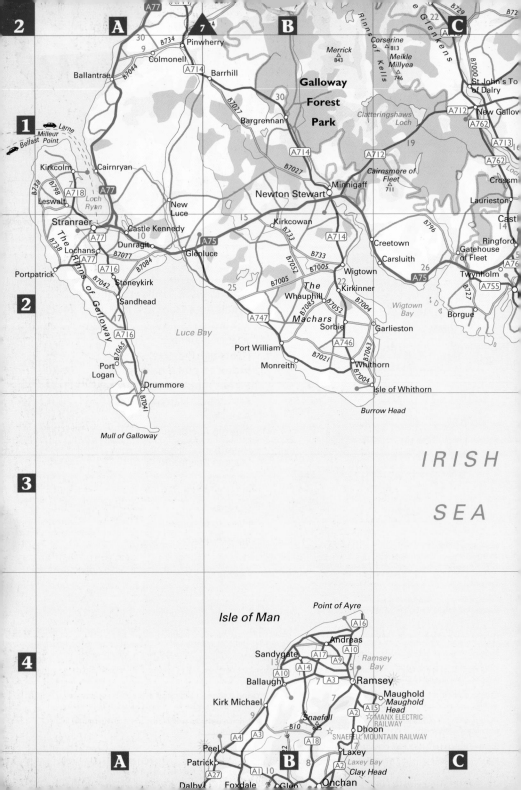

2

A | **B** | **C**

1

A77

B729 | B72

30 | B734 | Pinwherry

Colmonell | A714 | Barrhill

Ballantrae | B7044 | Barhill

Rinns of Kells

Merrick 843

Corserine 813

Meikle Millyea 746

Galloway Forest Park

B7027 | Bargrennan

Clatteringshaws Loch

St John's To of Dalry

A712 | New Gallov

A762

Larne | Milleur Point

Belfast

Kirkcolm

Cairnryan

A714

B7027 | Minnigaff

A712 | 19

Cairnsmore of Fleet 711

A713

A762

Crossm

Laurieston

Leswalt | Loch Ryan

New Luce

Newton Stewart

Cast

2

Stranraer | A77

Castle Kennedy | 10

Dunragit

New Luce

15 | Kirkcowan

B733

A714

Creetown

Carsluith

Ringford

Gatehouse of Fleet

Cast 14

The Rinns of Galloway | B738

Lochans | A77 | B7077 | B7084

Glenluce | A75

B7052 | B733

B7005

Wigtown

26 | A75

Twynholm

A76

A755

Portpatrick | B7042

Stoneykirk

Sandhead

B7005

25 | B7005

The Whauphill

A747

B7083 | B7052

Kirkinner

22

Sorbie

B7004

Wigtown Bay

B727

Borgue

Luce Bay

The Machars

Garlieston

A716

Port William

A746

Monreith | B7021

B7063

Whithorn

Port Logan

B1065

Drummore

B7041

B7004

Isle of Whithorn

Burrow Head

Mull of Galloway

IRISH

3

SEA

4

Point of Ayre

Isle of Man

A16

Andreas

A10

Sandygate | A17 | A9

13 | A14

Ramsey Bay

A10

Ballaugh | 7 | A3

Ramsey

Kirk Michael

9 | Snaefell 625

Maughold Maughold Head

A2 | A15

B10

MANX ELECTRIC RAILWAY

A18

Dhoon

SNAEFELL MOUNTAIN RAILWAY

A4 | A3

Peel

Patrick

Laxey

Laxey Bay

Clay Head

A1 | 10

Onchan

Dalby | Foxdale | Glen

A | **B** | **C**

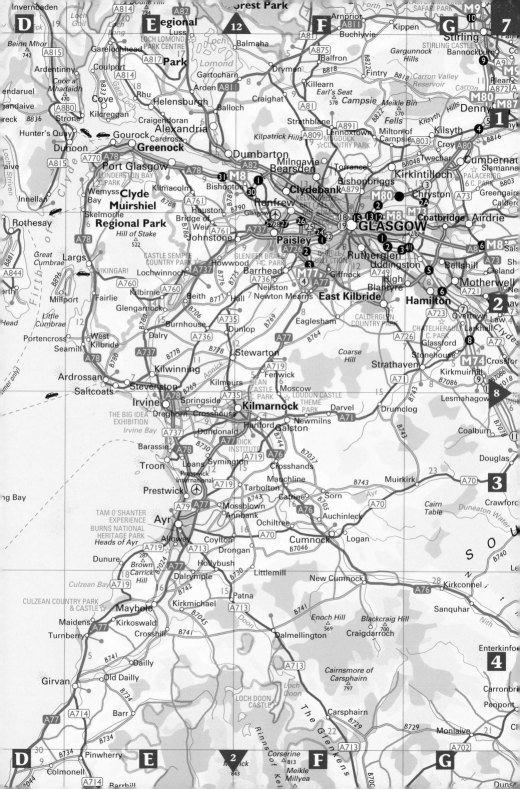

A

14

B   Rum
(Rhum)   Kinloch   Aird of Sleat

C

Point of Sl

Sound

1

Askival
812

Rubha nam
Meirleach

Cleadale

Eigg

An Sgurr
393   Galmisdale

Sound of Rum

Sound of Eigg

Sound of Ari

Lo

Castlebay

Eilean
nan Each

Muck

Castlebay

Lochboisdale

Sound of Ari

Eilean
Shona

I N N E R   H E B R I D E S

Point of
Ardnamurchan

Ockle   Ardtoe

Achosnich   Achara

A r d n a m u r c h a n

B8007   Ben Hiant
528

Kilchoan   Glenbeg
Glenborrodale

Eilean Mòr

Sorisdale

Clabhach   Coll

B8072
B8071

Arinagour

B8070

12   Loch
Eatharna

2

Ardmore Point

Caliach
Point   Calgary   Tobermory

Drimnin

Mo

Lo
Arien

B8073

Dervaig   Loch
Frisa   Killundine   B8849

Fiuna

Gunna

Crossapol
Bay

Calgary Bay

Kilninian

A848

SOUND OF MULL

Salen   A849

B8068   B8069   Caolas

Tiree   Scarinish

B8065

Barrapoll

Balephuil   Balemartine

Hynish Bay

ough Bay

Treshnish Isles

Gometra   Lagganulva
Ulva

Little
Colonsay

Staffa

Balnahard

Loch Tuath

B8073   B8035

Loch Na Keal

Ben More
966

Knock

Du
Gh

M u l l

23

Loch
Ba

3

B8035

Glen More   A

Ben Buie
717

IONA ABBEY
Baile Mòr
Iona   Fionnphort

Loch Scridain

Pennyghael   35

A849   Loch Buie

Sound of Iona

Bunessan

Carsaig

R o s s   o f   M u l l

Soa Island

Ardchiavaig

Malcolm's
Point

Fi

4

Garvel

Scar

Kiloran Bay

Rubh' a'Geodha

Colonsay   B8086   Kiloran

Kilchattan   Scalasaig

A

6

B   Gárvard

Loch Staosnaig

Dubh Eilean

C   inn Bhreac
467

Shian Bay

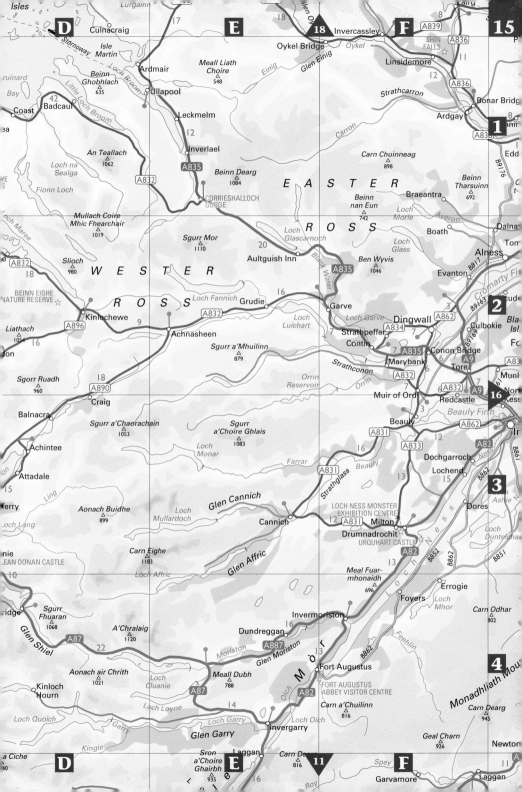

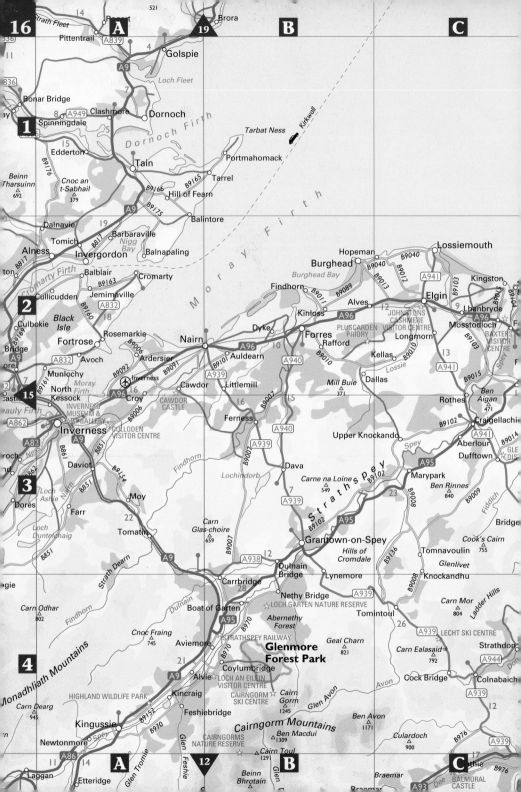

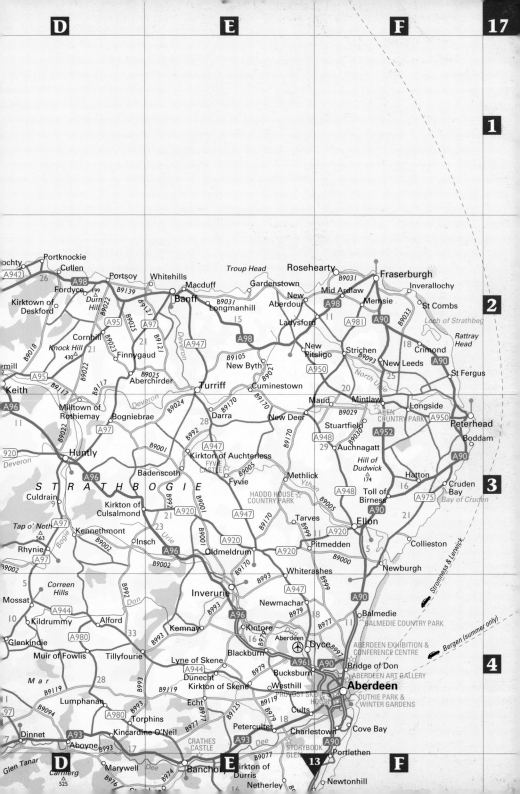

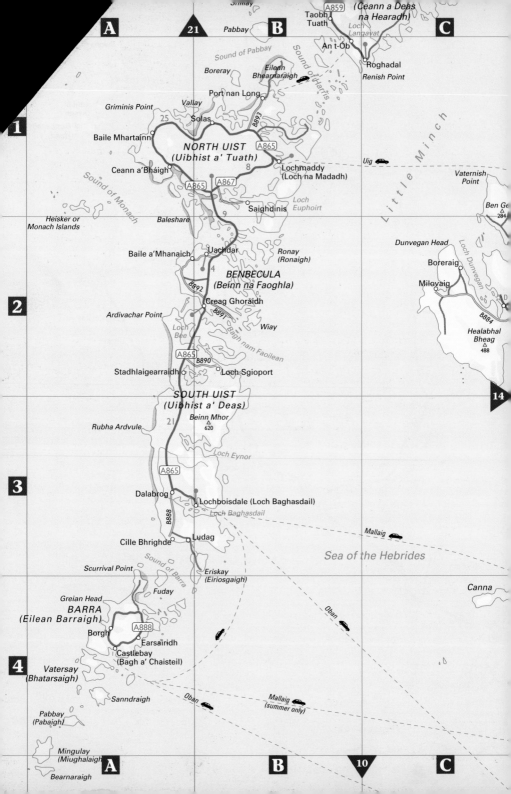

1

2

3

4

WESTERN
ISLES

Rubha
Robhanais

Eoropaidh
Tabost
Dail Bho
Thuath

Port Nis
Sgiogarstaigh

A857
15

Barabhas

Muirneag
△ 248

Tolastadh Úr
Tolsta Head

Arnol
Siabost
Bragar
A858
Carlabhagh

ISLE OF LEWIS
(Eilean Leodhais)

Beinn
Mholach
△ 292

A857

Griais

B895

East Loch Roag

West
Loch Roag

20

Tolastadh
a'Chaolais

Great
Bernera

Breascleit
Calanais

Miabhig
Crulabhig
B8059
Gearraidh na h-Aibhne

Stornoway
(Steornabhagh)
Newmarket

Loch a'
Tuath

Rubha an t-Siumpain
Port nan Giúran
Siulaisiadar

Timsgearraidh

Loch
Suainaval

Mealisval
△ 574

Einacleit
B8011

B8011

Achadh
Mór
13
A859
12

An Rubha
A866

Breanais

NORTH HARRIS
(Ceann a Tuath na Hearadh)

Baile Ailein

Crosbost
B897

Loch Erisort

Ullapool

alasta
Island

rp

Loch
Resort

Loch
Langavat
21

A859
Airidh
a'Bhruaich

B8060

Cearsiadar

Grabhair
B8060

Kebock Head

Huisinis

Tirga Mor
△ 679

B887

Abhainnsuidhe

Clishham
△ 799

A859

Beinn
Mhór
△ 572

Loch
Claidh

Loch
Shell

Leumrabhagh

Loch Seaforth

Taransay
(Taransaigh)

Aird
Asaig
A859

Tarbert
(An Tairbeart)

Loch
Bhrollum

Sound of Taransay

25

East Loch Tarbert

Gaolas Scalpaigh

Scalpay
(Eilean Scalpaigh)

Shiant Islands

3

Rubha

Me

Toe
ead

SOUTH
HARRIS
(Ceann a Deas
na Hearadh)

A859

Taobh
Tuath

Loch
Langavat

An t-Ób

Roghadal
Renish Point

Sound of Harris

Little Minch

Rubha Hunish

Kilmaluag

A855
19

Staffin Bay

4   He

Redp

hmaddy
ch na Madadh)

Loch
Euphoirt

Vaternish
Point

Ben Geary
△ 284

Balgown

Idrigil
Uig

Loch
Snizort

Staffin

A87
14

Culnaknock

Trotternish

Raasay

Fearnmo

Rona
A855
13

Fearn

D   E   F

A B C

1

**ORKNEY
ISLES**

Lerwick

Mull
Head

**Papa
Westray**

Noup Head

Pierowall

Westray

Skelwick

The North Sound

North Ronaldsay

Midbea

B9061

B9066

Burness

B9068

Broughtown

B9069

Overbister

Calfsound

Kettletoft

Sanday

2

Westray Firth

B9063

B9070

Rousay

Wasbister

B9064

Loth

Sanday
Sound

Westness

Brinian

Egilsay

Eday

Backaland

Brough Head

Birsay

18

Wyre

Whitehall

Stronsay

B9042

Twatt

A967

B9057

Tingwall

Gairsay

Egilsay

Aith

B9060

Rothiesholm

Skaill

B9056

Dounby

A966

Shapinsay

Stronsay
Firth

SKARA
BRAE

Loch of
Harray

A986

Bimbister

Balfour

B9058

Sandgarth

Wide
Firth

B9059

Auskerry

3

A967

B9055

A965

Finstown

A965

MAES
HOWE

7

Kirkwall

Scapa

Loch of
Stenness

9

Stromness

Graemsay

A964

Ward
Hill

Clestrain

19

Houton

Greenigo

13

Skaill

A960

Gritley

Ward Hill
479

Linksness

B9047

Scapa
Flow

A961

B9052

St Mary's

Copinsay

Hoy

Lyness

Flotta

Bow

20

Burray

St Margaret's Hope

Herston

Longhope

**South
Ronaldsay**

A961

Invergordon

South
Walls

Swona

Burwick

Cleat

4

Pentland Firth

Brough Ness

Pentland
Skerries

Stromness

Dunnet Head

Island of
Stroma

John o'
Groats

Aberdeen

Scrabster

Brough

A836

Mey

Dungansby
Head

A B 19 B C

Thurso

A836

Dunnet

Barrock

20

Freswick

A836

Castletown

Loch

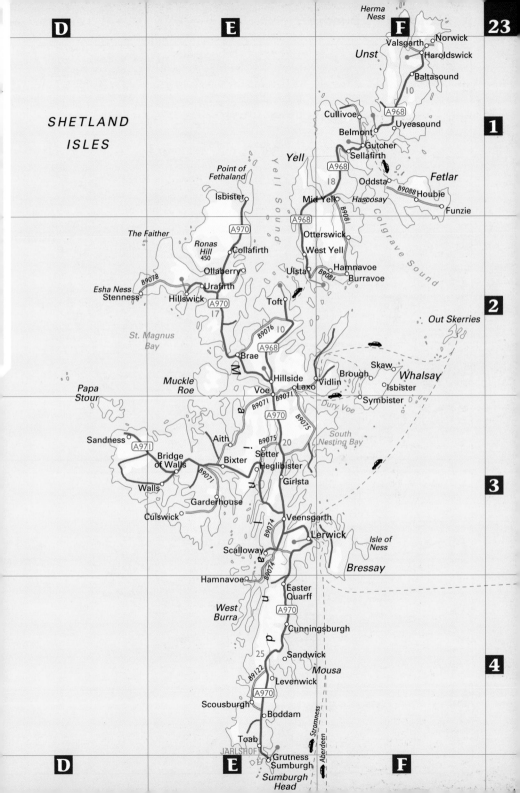

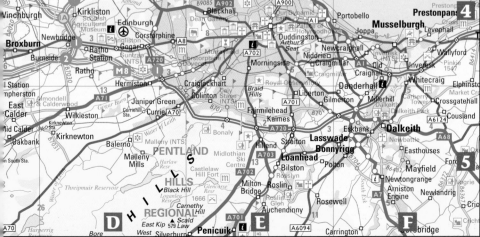

County Abbreviations

Aber.	Aberdeenshire	*E.Ayr.*	East Ayrshire	*Northumb.*	Northumberland
Arg. & B.	Argyll & Bute	*E.Dun.*	East Dunbartonshire	*Ork.*	Orkney
Cumb.	Cumbria	*Edin.*	Edinburgh	*P. & K.*	Perthshire & Kinross
D. & G.	Dumfries & Galloway	*High.*	Highland	*S.Ayr.*	South Ayrshire
Dur.	Durham	*Midloth.*	Midlothian	*S.Lan.*	South Lanarkshire
		N.Lan.	North Lanarkshire	*Sc.Bord.*	Scottish Borders
Shet.	Shetland				
Stir.	Stirling				
T. & W.	Tyne & Wear				
W.Dun.	West Dunbartonshire				
W. Loth.	West Lothian				

Note: Index entries shown in bold type can be found on the urban area maps, pages 24-25

A

Abbeytown	3 E2
Aberchirder	17 D2
Aberdeen	17 F4
Aberdeen	**24 C2**
Aberdeen Airport	17 E4
Aberdeen Airport	**24 B1**
Aberdour	8 B1
Aberfeldy	12 B2
Aberfoyle	12 A4
Aberlady	8 C1
Aberlemno	13 E2
Aberlour	16 C3
Abernethy	12 C4
Aberuthven	12 C4
Abhainnsuidhe	21 D3
Abington	8 A3
Aboyne	17 D4
Abronhill	**25 F1**
Achadh Mòr	21 E2
Achahoish	6 C1
Acharacle	10 C2
Achath	**24 A1**
Achavanich	19 E2
Achfary	18 B2
Achiltibuie	18 A3
Achintee	15 D3
Achnacroish	11 D3
Achnasheen	15 E2
Achosnich	10 C2
Achriesgill	18 B2
Acomb	4 B1
Aird Asaig	21 D3
Aird of Sleat	14 B4
Airdrie	7 G2
Airdrie	**25 F2**
Airidh a'Bhruaich	21 E2
Airth	8 A1
Aith *Ork.*	22 C2
Aith *Shet.*	23 E3
Akeld	9 E3
Alexandria	7 E1
Alford	17 D4
Allanton *N.Lan.*	8 A2
Allanton *S.Lan.*	**25 F3**
Allendale Town	4 B2
Allenheads	4 B2
Allnabad	18 C2
Alloa	12 B4
Allonby	3 E2
Alloway	7 E3
Alness	16 A2
Alnmouth	9 F4
Alnwick	9 F4
Alston	4 A2
Altens	**24 C2**
Altnafeadh	11 F2
Altnaharra	18 C2
Alva	12 B4
Alves	16 B2
Alvie	16 A4
Alyth	13 D2
Amble	9 F4
Ambleside	3 F4
Amulree	12 B3
An t-Ob	21 D4
An Tairbeart	21 E3
Ancroft	9 E2
Ancrum	9 D3
Andreas	2 B4
Annan	3 E1
Annbank	7 E3
Annfield Plain	4 C2
Anstruther	13 E4
Aoradh	6 A2
Appleby-in-Westmorland	4 A3
Applecross	14 C3
Arbirlot	13 E3

Arbroath	13 E3
Ardchiavaig	10 B4
Arden	7 E1
Ardentinny	7 E1
Ardeonaig	12 A3
Ardersier	16 A2
Ardfern	11 D4
Ardgay	18 C4
Ardlui	11 F4
Ardlussa	6 B1
Ardmair	18 A4
Ardminish	6 B2
Ardmolich	11 D1
Ardrishaig	6 C1
Ardrossan	7 E2
Ardtalnaig	12 A3
Ardtoe	10 C2
Ardvasar	14 C4
Arinagour	10 B2
Arisaig	10 C1
Armadale	8 A1
Arnisdale	14 C4
Arniston Engine	**25 F5**
Arnol	21 E1
Arnprior	12 A4
Arrochar	11 F4
Ashgill	**25 F3**
Ashington	5 D1
Ashkirk	8 C3
Aspatria	3 E2
Attadale	15 D3
Auchallater	12 C1
Auchenblae	13 E1
Auchenbreck	6 D1
Auchencairn	3 D2
Auchencrow	9 E2
Auchendinny	**25 E5**
Auchindrain	11 E4
Auchinleck	7 F3
Auchinloch	**25 E1**
Auchlunies	**24 B3**
Auchmull	13 E1
Auchnagatt	17 F3
Aucholzie	13 D1
Auchterarder	12 B4
Auchterhouse	**24 A4**
Auchtermuchty	13 D4
Auchtertool	8 B1
Auldearn	16 B2
Auldhouse	**25 E3**
Aultbea	15 D1
Aultguish Inn	15 E2
Aviemore	16 B4
Avoch	16 A2
Avonbridge	8 A1
Aycliffe	5 D3
Ayr	7 E3
Aysgarth	4 C4

B

Backaland	22 B2
Badcaul	18 A4
Badenscoth	17 E3
Badlipster	19 F2
Bagh a' Chaisteil (Castlebay)	20 A4
Baile a'Mhanaich	20 A2
Baile Ailein	21 E2
Baile Mhartainn	20 A1
Baile Mòr	10 B3
Bainbridge	4 B4
Balbeggie	12 C3
Balbithan	**24 A1**
Balblair	16 A2
Baldernock	**25 D1**
Baldovie	**24 B4**
Balemartine	10 A3
Balephuil	10 A3
Balerno	**25 D5**
Balfour	22 B3

Balfron	7 F1
Balgown	14 B2
Balgray	13 D3
Balgray	**24 B4**
Balhelvie	**24 A5**
Balintore	16 A2
Ballachulish	11 E2
Ballantrae	2 A1
Ballater	13 D1
Ballaugh	2 B4
Ballingry	12 C4
Ballinluig	12 C2
Ballintuim	12 C2
Balloch *N.Lan.*	**25 F1**
Balloch *W.Dun.*	7 E1
Ballochroy	6 C2
Ballygrant	6 A2
Balmacara	14 C3
Balmaha	7 E1
Balmedie	**24 C1**
Balmerino	**24 A5**
Balmore	**25 E1**
Balmullo	**24 B5**
Balnacra	15 D3
Balnahard	10 C3
Balnapaling	16 A2
Balquhidder	12 A3
Baltasound	23 F1
Balvicar	11 D4
Bamburgh	9 F3
Banchory	**24 A3**
Banchory-Devenick	**24 C2**
Banff	17 E2
Bankfoot	12 C3
Bankhead	**24 B2**
Bannockburn	8 A1
Barabhas	21 E1
Barassie	7 E3
Barbaraville	16 A2
Bargrennan	2 B1
Barnard Castle	4 C3
Barr	7 E4
Barrapoll	10 A3
Barrhead	7 F2
Barrhead	**25 D3**
Barrhill	2 B1
Barrock	19 F1
Barry	**24 C4**
Bathgate	8 A1
Beadnell	9 F3
Bearsden	7 F1
Bearsden	**25 D1**
Beattock	8 B4
Beauly	15 F3
Bedale	5 D4
Bedlington	4 C1
Beith	7 E2
Belford	9 F3
Belhelvie	**24 C1**
Bellingham	4 B1
Bellshill	7 G2
Bellshill	**25 F3**
Belmont	23 F1
Belsay	4 C1
Benthoul	**24 B2**
Benvie	**24 A4**
Bernisdale	14 B2
Berriedale	19 E3
Berwick-upon-Tweed	9 E2
Bettyhill	18 C1
Bieldside	**24 B2**
Biggar	8 A3
Bilbster	19 F2
Billingham	5 D3
Billy Row	4 C2
Bilston	8 B2
Bilston	**25 E5**

Bimbister	22 B3
Birkhill	**24 A4**
Birsay	22 A2
Birtley	5 D2
Bishop Auckland	4 C3
Bishopbriggs	**25 E2**
Bishopton	7 F1
Bixter	23 E3
Blackbraes	**24 B1**
Blackburn *Aber.*	17 E4
Blackburn *Aber.*	**24 B1**
Blackburn *W.Loth.*	8 A2
Blackchambers	**24 A1**
Blackdog	**24 C1**
Blackford	12 B4
Blackhall	**25 E4**
Blackhall Colliery	5 D2
Blacklunans	12 C2
Blackridge	8 A1
Blacktop	**24 B2**
Blackwaterfoot	6 C3
Blaich	11 E1
Blair Atholl	12 B2
Blairgowrie	12 C3
Blairdryne	**24 A3**
Blaydon	4 C1
Blyth	5 D1
Blyth Bridge	8 B2
Boat of Garten	16 B4
Boath	15 F2
Boddam *Aber.*	17 F3
Boddam *Shet.*	23 E4
Bogniebrae	17 D3
Bograxie	**24 A1**
Boldon	5 D2
Boltby	5 D4
Bolton	8 C1
Bonar Bridge	18 C4
Bonawe	11 E3
Bonawe Quarries	11 E3
Bonchester Bridge	9 D4
Bo'ness	8 A1
Bonjedward	9 D3
Bonnybridge	8 A1
Bonnyrigg	**25 F5**
Bonnyton *Angus*	**24 C4**
Bonnyton *Angus*	**24 A4**
Bootle	3 E4
Boreland	8 B4
Boreraig	14 A2
Borgh	20 A4
Borgue *D. & G.*	2 C2
Borgue *High.*	19 E3
Borrowdale	3 F3
Borrowfield	**24 B3**
Borve	14 B3
Bothel	3 E2
Bothwell	**25 F3**
Bottomcraig	**24 A5**
Bournemoor	5 D2
Bow	22 B4
Bowburn	5 D2
Bowes	4 B3
Bowmore	6 A2
Bowness-on-Solway	3 E1
Bowness-on-Windermere	3 F4
Bracadale	14 A3
Braco	12 B4
Bracora	11 D1
Brae	23 E2
Braeantra	15 F1
Braemar	12 C1
Bragar	21 E1
Braithwaite	3 E3
Brampton	4 A2
Brandon	4 C2

Breakish	14 C4
Breanais	21 D2
Breascleit	21 E2
Brechin	13 E2
Bridge of Allan	12 B4
Bridge of Balgie	12 A2
Bridge of Cally	12 C2
Bridge of Craigisla	13 D2
Bridge of Don	17 F4
Bridge of Don	**24 C2**
Bridge of Dun	13 E2
Bridge of Dye	13 E1
Bridge of Earn	12 C4
Bridge of Orchy	11 F3
Bridge of Walls	23 E3
Bridge of Weir	7 E2
Bridgend *Angus*	13 E2
Bridgend (Islay) *Arg. & B.*	6 A2
Bridgend (Lochgilphead) *Arg. & B.*	6 C1
Bridgend *Moray*	16 C3
Brig o'Turk	12 A4
Brigham	3 E3
Brinian	22 B2
Broadford	14 C4
Brochel	14 B3
Brodick	6 D3
Brompton	5 D4
Brompton on Swale	4 C4
Brora	19 D4
Brotton	5 E3
Brough *Cumb.*	4 B3
Brough *High.*	19 E1
Brough *Shet.*	23 F2
Broughton	8 B3
Broughton in Furness	3 E4
Broughtown	22 C2
Broughty Ferry	13 E3
Broughty Ferry	**24 B4**
Broxburn	8 B1
Brunton	**24 A5**
Buchlyvie	12 A4
Buckhaven	13 D4
Buckie	17 D2
Bucklerheads	**24 B4**
Bucksburn	17 E4
Bucksburn	**24 B2**
Buddon	**24 C4**
Buldoo	19 E1
Bunessan	10 B3
Burgh by Sands	3 F2
Burghead	16 B2
Burness	22 C2
Burnhervie	**24 A1**
Burnhouse	7 E2
Burniston	5 F4
Burnmouth	9 E2
Burnopfield	4 C2
Burnside	**24 A1**
Burnside of Duntrune	**24 B4**
Burntisland	8 B1
Burravoe	23 F2
Burrelton	12 C3
Burwick	22 B4
Busby	**25 D3**
Buttermere	3 E3

C

Cadder	25 E1
Cairnbaan	6 C1
Cairndow	11 E4
Cairneyhill	8 A1
Cairnie	**24 B2**
Cairnryan	2 A1
Calanais	21 E2
Caldbeck	3 F2

Place	Page	Ref
Calderbank	25	F2
Caldercruix	8	A1
Calderglen	25	E3
Caldwell	4	C3
Calfsound	22	B2
Calgary	10	B2
Callander	12	A4
Calvine	12	B2
Camasnacroise	11	D2
Cambuslang	25	E2
Cammachmore	24	C3
Campbeltown	6	C3
Camptown	9	D4
Cannich	15	E3
Canonbie	3	F1
Caolas	10	A2
Caolas Scalpaigh	21	E3
Cappercleuch	8	B3
Capplegill	8	B4
Caputh	12	C3
Carbost (Loch Harport) High.	14	B3
Carbost (Loch Snizort Beag) High.	14	B3
Carbrain	25	F1
Cardenden	13	D4
Cardross	7	E1
Cargenbridge	3	D1
Cargill	12	C3
Carlabhagh	21	E1
Carlisle	3	F2
Carlops	8	B2
Carluke	8	A2
Carmunnock	25	E3
Carmyle	25	E2
Carmyllie	13	E3
Carnbee	13	E4
Carnbo	12	C4
Carnoustie	13	E3
Carnoustie	24	C4
Carnwath	8	A2
Carradale	6	C3
Carrbridge	16	B4
Carrick	24	B5
Carrington	25	F5
Carronbridge	8	A4
Carsaig	10	C3
Carsluith	2	C2
Carsphairn	7	F4
Carstairs	8	A2
Castle Carrock	4	A2
Castle Douglas	3	D2
Castle Kennedy	2	A2
Castlebay (Bagh a' Chaisteil)	20	A4
Castlemilk	25	E3
Castleside	4	C2
Castleton	5	E4
Castletown	19	E1
Catrine	7	F3
Catterick	4	C4
Catterick Camp	4	C4
Causeyend	24	C1
Cawdor	16	A2
Ceann a'Bháigh	20	A1
Cearsiadar	21	E2
Ceres	13	D4
Champany	8	A1
Chapelhall	25	F2
Charlestown	17	F4
Charlestown	24	C2
Chatton	9	E3
Chester-le-Street	5	D1
Chesters	9	D4
Chilton	5	D3
Chirnside	9	E2
Chopwell	4	C1
Christon Bank	9	F3
Chryston	7	G1
Chryston	25	E1
Cille Bhrighde	20	A4
Clabhach	10	A2
Clachan (Kintyre) Arg. & B.	6	C2
Clachan (Loch Fyne) Arg. & B.	11	E4
Clachan (Raasay) High.	14	B3
Clachan of Glendaruel	6	D1
Clachtoll	18	A3
Clackmannan	8	A1
Cladich	11	E3
Claggan	11	D2
Claonaig	6	C2
Clarkston	25	D3
Clashmore	16	A1
Clashnessie	18	A3
Cleadale	10	C1
Cleadon	5	D1
Cleat	22	B4
Cleator Moor	3	E3
Cleland	8	A2
Cleland	25	F3
Clestrain	22	A3
Clinterty	24	B1
Closeburn	8	A4
Cloughton	5	F4
Clova	13	D1
Clovenfords	8	C3
Clovenstone	24	A1
Cloverhill	24	C1
Clovullin	11	E2
Clunes	11	E1
Clydebank	7	F1
Clydebank	25	D2
Coalburn	8	A3
Coast	15	D1
Coatbridge	7	G2
Coatbridge	25	F2
Cock Bridge	16	C4
Cockburnspath	9	D1
Cockenzie & Port Seton	8	C1
Cockermouth	3	E3
Cockfield	4	C3
Coldingham	9	E2
Coldstream	9	E3
Colinton	25	E5
Colintraive	6	D1
Collafirth	23	E2
Collieston	17	F3
Collin	3	E1
Colmonell	2	A1
Colnabaichin	16	C4
Colquhar	8	C2
Comrie	12	B3
Condorrat	25	F1
Coniston	3	F4
Connel	11	D3
Conon Bridge	15	F2
Consett	4	C2
Contin	15	F2
Contlaw	24	B2
Cookney	24	B3
Copley	4	C3
Corbridge	4	B1
Cornhill	17	D2
Cornhill-on-Tweed	9	E3
Corpach	11	E1
Corrie	6	D2
Corsock	3	D1
Corstorphine	25	D4
Coshieville	12	B2
Cothall	24	B1
Cottown	24	A1
Coulport	7	E1
Coultra	24	A5
Coundon	4	C3
Coupar Angus	13	D3
Cousland	25	F5
Cove Arg. & B.	7	E1
Cove High.	14	C1
Cove Bay	17	F4
Cove Bay	24	C2
Cowdenbeath	8	B1
Cowie	8	A1
Cowshill	4	B2
Coylton	7	E3
Coylumbridge	16	B4
Craibstone	24	B1
Craichie	13	E2
Craig	15	D3
Craigandaive	7	D1
Craigdarroch	7	F4
Craigearn	24	A1
Craigellachie	16	C3
Craigendoran	7	E1
Craighat	7	F1
Craigie	24	C1
Craiglockhart	25	E4
Craiglug	24	B3
Craigmillar	25	E4
Craignure	11	D3
Craigton	24	B2
Aberdeen		
Craigton Angus	24	C4
Crail	13	E4
Cramlington	5	D1
Cramond	8	B1
Cramond	25	D4
Cranshaws	9	D2
Crask Inn	18	C3
Craster	9	F3
Crathes	24	A3
Crathie	13	D1
Crawfordjohn	8	A3
Creag Ghoraidh	20	B2
Creetown	2	C2
Creich	24	A5
Crianlarich	11	F3
Crichton	25	F5
Crieff	12	B3
Crimond	17	F2
Crinan	11	D4
Crocketford or Ninemile Bar	3	D1
Cromarty	16	A2
Crook	4	C3
Crookham	9	E3
Crosbost	21	E2
Crosby Ravensworth	4	A3
Crossaig	6	C2
Crosscanonby	3	E2
Crossford Fife	8	B1
Crossford S.Lan.	8	A2
Crossgatehall	25	F5
Crossgates	8	B1
Crosshands	7	F3
Crosshill	7	E4
Crosshouse	7	E3
Crossmichael	2	C1
Crossroads	24	A3
Croy High.	16	A3
Croy N.Lan.	7	G1
Croy N.Lan.	25	F1
Cruden Bay	17	F3
Crulabhig	21	E2
Crutherland	25	E3
Culbokie	15	F2
Culdrain	17	D3
Cullen	17	D2
Cullicudden	16	A2
Cullipool	11	D4
Cullivoe	23	F1
Culnacraig	18	A4
Culnaknock	14	B2
Culross	8	A1
Culswick	23	E3
Cults	17	E4
Cults	24	B2
Cumbernauld	7	G1
Cumbernauld	25	F1
Cuminestown	17	E2
Cumnock	7	F3
Cunningsburgh	23	E4
Cupar	13	D4
Currie	25	D5

D

Place	Page	Ref
Dacre	3	F3
Dail Bho Thuath	21	F1
Dailly	7	E4
Dairsie	13	D4
Dalabrog	20	A3
Dalbeattie	3	D2
Dalgety Bay	8	B1
Dalkeith	8	C1
Dalkeith	25	F5
Dallas	16	B2
Dalmadilly	24	A1
Dalmally	11	E3
Dalmellington	7	F4
Dalmeny	25	D4
Dalnavie	16	A2
Dalry	7	E2
Dalrymple	7	E4
Dalserf	25	F3
Dalston	3	F1
Dalwhinnie	12	A1
Danby	5	E4
Danderhall	25	F5
Danestone	24	C1
Darlington	5	D3
Darnford	24	A3
Darra	17	E3
Darvel	7	F3
Dava	16	B3
Daviot	16	A3
Dearham	3	E3
Dechmont	8	A1
Denhead Aber.	24	A1
Denhead Dundee	24	A4
Denholm	9	D3
Denmill	24	B1
Denny	8	A1
Denside	24	B3
Dervaig	10	C2
Dhoon	2	B4
Dingwall	15	F2
Dinnet	17	D4
Dippen	6	C3
Dirleton	8	C1
Distington	3	E3
Dochgarroch	15	F3
Doddington	9	E3
Dollar	12	B4
Dolphinton	8	B2
Dores	15	F3
Dornie	15	D3
Dornoch	16	A1
Dougalston	25	D1
Dougarie	6	C3
Douglas	8	A3
Douglas & Angus	24	B4
Douglastown	13	D2
Dounby	22	A3
Doune	12	B4
Dounreay	19	E1
Dowally	12	C2
Downfield	24	A4
Downies	24	C3
Dreghorn	7	E3
Drem	8	C1
Drimnin	10	C2
Drongan	7	F3
Dronley	24	A4
Druimdrishaig	6	C1
Drumbeg	18	A3
Drumchapel	25	D1
Drumclog	7	F3
Drumlithie	13	F1
Drummore	2	A2
Drumnadrochit	15	F3
Drumoak	24	A3
Drumsturdy	24	B4
Drymen	7	F1
Duddingston	25	E4
Duddo	9	E2
Dufftown	16	C3
Duirinish	14	C3
Dullatur	25	F1
Dulnain Bridge	16	B3
Dumbarton	7	E1
Dumfries	3	D1
Dunbar	9	D1
Dunbeath	19	E3
Dunblane	12	B4
Dundee	13	D3
Dundee	24	B4
Dundee Airport	24	A5
Dundonald	7	E3
Dundreggan	15	E4
Dundrennan	3	D2
Dunecht	17	E4
Dunecht	24	A2
Dunfermline	8	B1
Dunkeld	12	C3
Dunlop	7	E2
Dunnet	19	E1
Dunning	12	C4
Dunoon	7	E1
Dunragit	2	A2
Duns	9	D2
Dunscore	3	D1
Dunure	7	E3
Dunvegan	14	A3
Durham	5	D2
Durness	18	B1
Dyce	17	E4
Dyce	24	B1
Dyke	16	B2
Dykehead	13	D2

E

Place	Page	Ref
Eaglescliffe	5	D3
Eaglesfield	3	E1
Eaglesham	7	F2
Eaglesham	25	D3
Earlston	9	D3
Earsairidh	20	A4
Easdale	11	D4
Easington	5	D2
Easington Colliery	5	D2
East Auchronie	24	B2
East Calder	8	B1
East Haven	13	E3
East Haven	24	C4
East Kilbride	7	F2
East Kilbride	25	E3
East Linton	9	D1
East March	24	B4
East Wemyss	13	D4
Easter Lednathie	13	D2
Easter Ord	24	B2
Easter Quarff	23	E4
Eastgate	4	B2
Easthouses	25	F5
Eastriggs	3	F1
Ecclaw	9	D1
Ecclefechan	3	E1
Eccles	9	D2
Echt	17	E4
Echt	24	A2
Eckford	9	D3
Edderton	16	A1
Eddleston	8	B2
Eddlewood	25	F3
Edinbarnet	25	D1
Edinburgh	8	B1
Edinburgh	25	E4
Edinburgh Airport	8	B1
Edinburgh Airport	25	D4
Edlingham	9	F4
Edmundbyers	4	C2
Edzell	13	E2
Egglescliffe	5	D3
Egglingham	9	F3
Egremont	3	E3
Egton	5	F4
Einacleit	21	D2
Elgin	16	C2
Elgol	14	B4
Elie	13	E4
Ellingham	9	F3
Ellington	9	F4
Ellon	17	F3
Elphin	18	B3
Elphinstone	25	F4
Elrick	24	B2
Elsdon	9	E4
Elsrickle	8	B2
Elvanfoot	8	A3
Embleton	9	F3
Enterkinfoot	8	A4
Eoropaidh	21	F1
Eriboll	18	B2
Errogie	15	F4
Errol	13	D3
Esh Winning	4	C2
Eskbank	25	F5
Eskdalemuir	8	B4
Eston	5	E3
Etteridge	12	A1
Ettrick	8	B4
Ettrickbridge	8	C3
Evanton	16	A2
Eyemouth	9	E2

F

Place	Page	Ref
Faifley	25	D1
Fairholm	25	F3
Fairley	24	B2
Fairlie	7	E2
Fairmilehead	25	E5
Falkirk	8	A1
Falkland	13	D4
Fallin	8	A1
Falstone	4	A1
Farr	16	A3
Fauldhouse	8	A2
Fearnmore	14	C2
Felling	5	D1
Felton	9	F4
Fenwick E.Ayr.	7	F2
Fenwick Northumb.	9	F2
Feochaig	6	C4
Feolin Ferry	6	B1
Fern	13	E2
Ferness	16	B3
Ferryden	13	E2
Ferryhill	5	D3

Place	Map	Grid
Feshiebridge	16	A4
Fettercairn	13	E1
Fetternear House	24	A1
Finavon	13	E2
Findhorn	16	B2
Findochty	17	D2
Findon	24	C3
Finnygaud	17	D2
Finstown	22	B3
Fintry	7	F1
Fionnphort	10	B3
Fishburn	5	D3
Fishnish	10	C3
Fiunary	10	C2
Flemington	25	E3
Flimby	3	E3
Flodden	9	E3
Fochabers	16	C2
Ford *Arg. & B.*	11	D4
Ford *Midloth.*	25	F5
Ford *Northumb.*	13	F1
Fordoun	13	F1
Fordyce	17	D2
Forfar	13	D2
Forgandenny	12	C3
Forgie	16	C2
Forres	16	B2
Forsinard	19	D2
Fort Augustus	15	E4
Fort William	11	E1
Forth	8	A2
Fortingall	12	B2
Fortrose	16	A2
Foulden	9	E2
Fowlis	24	A4
Foyers	15	F4
Fraserburgh	17	F2
Freswick	19	F1
Freuchie	13	D4
Friockheim	13	E2
Frizington	3	E3
Funzie	23	F1
Furnace	11	E4
Fyvie	17	E3
G		
Gainford	4	C3
Gairloch	14	C1
Galashiels	8	C3
Galmisdale	10	C1
Galston	7	F3
Gardenstown	17	E2
Garderhouse	23	E3
Garelochhead	7	E1
Garlieston	2	C2
Garlogie	24	A2
Garsdale Head	4	B4
Gartcosh	25	E2
Gartocharn	7	F1
Garvald	9	D1
Garvamore	12	A1
Garvard	6	A1
Garve	16	A2
Gatehouse of Fleet	2	C2
Gateshead	5	D2
Gauldry	24	A5
Gawthrop	4	A4
Gearraidh na h-Aibhne	21	E2
Giffnock	7	F2
Giffnock	25	D3
Gifford	8	C1
Gillamoor	5	E4
Gilling West	4	C3
Gilmerton *Edin.*	25	E5
Gilmerton *P. & K.*	12	B3
Gilsland	4	A1
Gilston	8	C2
Girlsta	23	E3
Girvan	7	E4
Glamis	13	D2
Glanton	9	F3
Glasgow	7	F2
Glasgow	25	D2
Glasgow Airport	7	F2
Glashmore	24	A2
Glassford	7	G2
Glenbarr	6	C3
Glenbeg	10	C2
Glenboig	25	F2
Glenborrodale	10	C2
Glenbreck	8	B3
Glenbrittle	14	B4
Glencaple	3	E1
Glencarse	12	C3
Glencoe	11	E2
Gleneagles	12	B4
Glenegedale	6	A2
Glenelg	14	C4
Glenfarg	12	C4
Glenfinnan	11	D1
Glengarnock	7	E2
Glenkindie	17	D4
Glenluce	2	A2
Glenmavis	25	F2
Glenrothes	13	D4
Gogar	25	D4
Golspie	19	D4
Gordon	9	D2
Gorebridge	25	F5
Gosforth *Cumb.*	3	E4
Gosforth *T. & W.*	4	C1
Gourdon	13	F2
Govan	25	D2
Grabhair	21	E2
Grandtully	12	B2
Grangemouth	8	A1
Grantlodge	24	A1
Grantown-on-Spey	16	B3
Grantshouse	9	D2
Grasmere	3	F4
Grayrigg	4	A4
Great Ayton	5	E3
Great Broughton	5	E4
Great Clifton	3	E3
Great Salkeld	4	A2
Greenburn	24	B4
Greengairs	7	G1
Greengairs	25	F1
Greenhead	4	A1
Greenigo	22	B3
Greenlaw	9	D2
Greenloaning	12	B4
Greenock	7	E1
Gretna	3	F1
Greystoke	3	F3
Griais	21	F1
Gritley	22	B3
Grizebeck	3	E4
Grudie	15	E2
Grutness	23	E4
Guide Post	4	C1
Guildtown	12	C3
Guisborough	5	E3
Gullane	8	C1
Gutcher	23	F1
H		
Hackness	5	F4
Haddington	8	C1
Halkirk	19	E2
Hall	7	E2
Haltwhistle	4	A1
Ham	23	D3
Hamilton	7	G2
Hamilton	25	F3
Hamnavoe (Mainland) *Shet.*	23	E4
Hamnavoe (Yell) *Shet.*	23	F2
Hardgate	24	A2
Haroldswick	23	F1
Harrietfield	12	C3
Harthill	8	A2
Hartlepool	5	E3
Hassendean	8	C3
Haswell	5	D2
Hatton	17	F3
Hatton of Fintray	24	A1
Haugh of Urr	3	D1
Hawes	4	B4
Hawick	8	C3
Hawkshead	3	F4
Haydon Bridge	4	B1
Hazelhead	24	B2
Hazelton Walls	24	A5
Healeyfield	4	C2
Heathcot	24	B2
Hebburn	5	D1
Heglibister	23	E3
Helensburgh	7	E1
Helmsdale	19	E3
Helmsley	5	E4
Heriot	8	C2
Hermiston	25	D4
Herston	22	B4
Hetton-le-Hole	5	D2
Hexham	4	B1
High Blantyre	7	G2
High Blantyre	25	E3
High Etherley	4	C3
High Hawsker	5	F4
High Hesket	3	F2
High Lorton	3	E3
Hill End	12	C4
Hill of Fearn	16	A1
Hillend	25	E5
Hillside *Aber.*	24	C3
Hillside *Angus*	13	E2
Hillside *Shet.*	23	E2
Hillswick	23	E2
Hinderwell	5	F3
Hirn	24	A2
Hollybush	7	E3
Holytown	25	F2
Holywood	3	D1
Hopeman	16	B2
Horden	5	D2
Houbie	23	F1
Houghton le Spring	5	D2
Houndslow	9	D2
Houston	7	E2
Houton	22	B3
Howwood	7	E2
Huisinis	21	D3
Humbie	8	C2
Hunter's Quay	7	E1
Huntly	17	D3
Hurlford	7	F3
Hurworth-on-Tees	5	D3
Hutton Rudby	5	D4
I		
Idrigill	14	B2
Inchbare	13	E2
Inchnadamph	18	B3
Inchture	13	D3
Ingleton	4	C3
Innellan	7	D1
Innerleithen	8	C3
Insch	17	D3
Inveralligan	14	C2
Inverallochy	17	F2
Inveraray	11	D3
Inverarity	11	H4
Inverbervie	13	F1
Invercassley	18	C4
Invercharnan	11	E2
Inveresk	25	F4
Inverey	12	C1
Invergarry	15	E4
Invergordon	16	A2
Invergowrie	24	A4
Inverinan	11	E4
Inverkeilor	13	E2
Inverkeithing	8	B1
Inverkirkaig	18	A3
Inverlael	15	E1
Invermoriston	15	F4
Inverneil	6	C1
Inverness	16	A2
Inverness Airport	16	A2
Invernoaden	11	E4
Inverurie	17	E4
Irvine	7	E3
Isbister (Mainland) *Shet.*	23	E1
Isbister (Whalsay) *Shet.*	23	F2
Isle of Whithorn	2	C2
J		
Jackton	25	D3
Jarrow	5	D1
Jedburgh	9	D3
Jemimaville	16	A2
John o' Groats	19	F1
Johnstone	7	F2
Johnstonebridge	8	B4
Joppa	25	F4
Juniper Green	25	D5
K		
Kaimes	25	E5
Kames	6	D1
Keillmore	6	C1
Keiss	19	F1
Keith	17	D2
Kellas *Angus*	13	D3
Kellas *Angus*	24	B4
Kellas *Moray*	16	C2
Kelso	9	D3
Kelty	12	C4
Kemnay	17	E4
Kemnay	24	A1
Kenmore	12	B2
Kennacraig	6	C2
Kennethmont	17	D3
Kennoway	13	D4
Kensaleyre	14	B2
Kentallen	11	E2
Keswick	3	F3
Kettletoft	22	C2
Kielder	9	D4
Kilberry	6	C2
Kilbirnie	7	E2
Kilcadzow	8	A2
Kilchattan	10	B4
Kilchenzie	6	C3
Kilchiaran	6	A3
Kilchoan	10	C2
Kilchoman	6	A3
Kilchrenan	11	E3
Kilconquhar	13	E4
Kilcreggan	7	E1
Kildonan Lodge	19	D3
Kildrummy	17	D4
Kilfinan	6	D1
Kilham	9	E3
Killean	6	C2
Killearn	7	F1
Killichonan	12	A2
Killiecrankie	12	B2
Killin	12	A3
Killingworth	5	D1
Killundine	10	C2
Kilmacolm	7	E1
Kilmalieu	11	D2
Kilmaluag	14	B2
Kilmany	24	A5
Kilmarnock	7	F3
Kilmartin	11	D4
Kilmaurs	7	F3
Kilmelford	11	D4
Kilmory *Arg. & B.*	6	C1
Kilmory (Rum) *High.*	14	A4
Kilninian	10	B2
Kilninver	11	D3
Kiloran	10	B4
Kilrenny	13	E4
Kilsyth	7	G1
Kilwinning	7	E2
Kinbrace	19	D3
Kincardine	11	F4
Kincardine O'Neil	17	D4
Kincorth	24	C2
Kincraig	16	A4
Kinellar	24	B1
Kingarth	7	D2
Kinghorn	8	B1
Kinglassie	13	D4
Kingoodie	24	A5
Kingsbarns	13	E4
Kingsford	24	B2
Kingshouse	12	A3
Kingston	16	C2
Kingswells	24	B2
Kingussie	16	A4
Kinkell	25	E1
Kinloch	14	B4
Kinloch Hourn	15	D4
Kinloch Rannoch	12	A2
Kinlochard	12	A4
Kinlochbervie	18	B2
Kinlochcheil	11	E1
Kinlochewe	15	D2
Kinlochleven	11	E2
Kinloss	16	B2
Kinmuck	24	B1
Kinross	12	C4
Kintore	17	E4
Kintore	24	A1
Kintour	6	B2
Kintra	6	A2
Kirkbride	3	E2
Kirkby Stephen	4	B4
Kirkbymoorside	5	E4
Kirkcaldy	8	B1
Kirkcolm	2	A1
Kirkconnel	7	G4
Kirkcowan	2	B2
Kirkcudbright	2	C2
Kirkinner	2	B2
Kirkintilloch	7	F1
Kirkintilloch	25	E1
Kirkliston	8	B1
Kirkliston	25	D4
Kirkmichael *P. & K.*	12	C2
Kirkmichael *S.Ayr.*	7	E4
Kirkmuirhill	8	A2
Kirknewton *Northumb.*	9	E3
Kirknewton *W.Loth.*	8	B1
Kirknewton *W.Loth.*	25	D5
Kirkoswald *Cumb.*	4	A2
Kirkoswald *S.Ayr.*	7	E4
Kirkpatrick Durham	3	D1
Kirkpatrick-Fleming	3	F1
Kirkton *Arg. & B.*	11	D4
Kirkton *Fife*	24	A5
Kirkton of Auchterhouse	24	A4
Kirkton of Culsalmond	17	D3
Kirkton of Durris	13	F1
Kirkton of Durris	24	A3
Kirkton of Glenisla	13	D2
Kirkton of Kingoldrum	13	D2
Kirkton of Maryculter	24	B3
Kirkton of Menmuir	13	E2
Kirkton of Monikie	24	C4
Kirkton of Skene	17	E4
Kirkton of Skene	24	B2
Kirkton of Strathmartine	24	A4
Kirkton of Tealing	24	B4
Kirktown of Auchterless	17	E3
Kirktown of Deskford	17	D2
Kirkwall	22	B3
Kirriemuir	13	D2
Knayton	5	D4
Knock	10	C3
Knockandhu	16	C4
Kyle of Lochalsh	14	C3
Kyleakin	14	C3
Kylerhea	14	C4
Kylestrome	18	B2
L		
Ladybank	13	D4
Ladykirk	9	E2
Ladysford	17	E2
Lagg	6	D3
Laggan (Invergarry) *High.*	11	F1
Laggan (Newtonmore) *High.*	12	A1
Lagganulva	10	C3
Laide	15	D1
Lairg	18	C4
Lamlash	6	D3
Lanark	8	A2
Lanchester	4	C2
Landerberry	24	A2
Langholm	3	F1
Langwathby	4	A3
Larbert	8	A1
Largoward	13	D4
Largs	7	E2
Larkhall	7	G2
Larkhall	25	F3
Lasswade	25	F5
Latheron	19	E2
Latheronwheel	19	E3
Lauchintilly	24	A1
Lauder	8	C2
Laurencekirk	13	E2
Laurieston	2	C1
Law	8	A2
Lawers	12	A3

Name	Pg	Ref
Laws	24	**B4**
Laxey	2	B4
Laxford Bridge	18	B2
Laxo	23	E2
Lazonby	4	A2
Leadburn	8	B2
Leadgate	4	C2
Leadhills	8	A3
Leckmelm	15	E1
Ledaig	11	D3
Ledmore	18	B3
Leeming	5	D4
Leith	8	B1
Leith	25	**E4**
Lennoxtown	7	F1
Lenzie	25	**E1**
Leoch	24	**A4**
Lerwick	23	E3
Lesbury	9	F4
Leschangie	24	**A1**
Leslie	13	D4
Lesmahagow	8	A3
Leswalt	2	A1
Leuchars	13	D3
Leuchars	24	**B5**
Leumrabhagh	21	E3
Leven	13	D4
Levenhall	25	**F4**
Levenwick	23	E4
Leyburn	4	C4
Leylodge	24	**A1**
Lhanbryde	16	C2
Libberton	8	A2
Liberton	25	**E5**
Liff	24	**A4**
Lilliesleaf	8	C3
Limekilburn	25	**F3**
Limekilns	8	B1
Lindores	13	D4
Linksness	22	A3
Linlithgow	8	A1
Linsidemore	15	F1
Littlemill *E.Ayr.*	7	F3
Littlemill *High.*	16	B2
Livingston	8	B1
Loanhead	8	B2
Loanhead	25	**E5**
Loans	7	E3
Loch Baghasdail (Lochboisdale)	20	B3
Loch na Madadh (Lochmaddy)	20	B1
Loch Sgioport	20	B2
Lochailort	11	D1
Lochaline	10	C3
Lochans	2	A2
Locharbriggs	3	E1
Lochawe	11	E3
Lochboisdale (Loch Baghasdail)	20	B3
Lochcarron	15	D3
Lochdon	11	D3
Lochearnhead	12	A3
Lochee	24	**A4**
Lochend	15	F3
Lochgelly	12	C4
Lochgilphead	6	C1
Lochgoilhead	11	F4
Lochinver	18	A3
Lochmaben	3	E1
Lochmaddy (Loch na Madadh)	20	B1
Lochranza	6	D2
Lochwinnoch	7	E2
Lockerbie	3	E1
Lockton	5	F4
Loftus	5	E3
Logan	7	F3
Logie	24	**B5**
Longbenton	5	D1
Longdrum	24	**C1**
Longforgan	13	D3
Longforgan	24	**A5**
Longframlington	9	F4
Longhope	22	A4
Longhorsley	9	F4
Longhoughton	9	F3
Longmanhill	17	E2
Longmorn	16	C2
Longniddry	8	C1
Longside	17	F3
Longtown	3	F1
Lossiemouth	16	C2
Loth	22	C2
Lothmore	19	E3
Low Waters	25	**F3**
Lower Diabaig	14	C2
Lower Killeyan	6	A4
Loweswater	3	E3
Lowick	9	E3
Lucklawhill	24	**B5**
Ludag	20	A3
Luggiebank	25	**F1**
Luib	14	B3
Lumphanan	17	D4
Luncarty	12	C3
Lundin Links	13	D4
Luss	7	E1
Lusta	14	A2
Lybster	19	F2
Lymekilns	25	**E3**
Lyne	24	**A2**
Lyne of Skene	17	E4
Lyne of Skene	24	**A1**
Lynemore	16	B3
Lynemouth	9	F4
Lyness	22	A4

M

Name	Pg	Ref
Macduff	17	E2
Machan	25	**F3**
Macharioch	6	C4
Machrihanish	6	B3
Macmerry	8	C1
Maidens	7	E4
Mains of Ardestie	24	**C4**
Mains of Drum	24	**B2**
Mains of Linton	24	**A2**
Mallaig	10	C1
Malleny Mills	25	**D5**
Malletsheugh	25	**D3**
Mannofield	24	**C2**
Markinch	13	D4
Marske-by-the-Sea	5	E3
Marybank	15	F2
Maryhill	25	**D2**
Marykirk	13	E2
Marypark	16	C3
Maryport	3	E3
Marywell (Deeside) *Aber.*	13	E1
Marywell (Portlethen) *Aber.*	24	**C3**
Mastrick	24	**B2**
Mauchline	7	F3
Maud	17	F3
Maughold	2	C4
Maybole	7	E4
Mayfield	25	**F5**
Mealsgate	3	E2
Mearns	25	**D3**
Meigle	13	D3
Meikle Earnock	25	**F3**
Meikle Kilmory	7	D2
Meikleour	12	C3
Melmerby	4	A2
Melrose	8	C3
Melsonby	4	C4
Melvaig	14	C1
Melvich	19	D1
Memsie	17	F2
Menstrie	12	B4
Methlick	17	E3
Methven	12	C3
Mey	19	F1
Miabhig	21	D2
Mickleton	4	B3
Mid Ardlaw	17	F2
Mid Yell	23	F1
Midbea	22	B2
Middleham	4	C4
Middlesbrough	5	D3
Middleton	24	**B1**
Middleton-in-Teesdale	4	B3
Middleton of Potterton	24	**C1**
Middleton Park	24	**C1**
Midlem	8	C3
Milfield	9	E3
Mill of Monquich	24	**B3**
Millden	24	**C1**
Millerhill	25	**F5**
Millhouse	6	D1
Millport	7	D2
Milltimber	24	**B2**
Milltown of Rothiemay	17	D3
Milnathort	12	C4
Milngavie	7	F1
Milngavie	25	**D1**
Milovaig	14	A2
Milton *High.*	15	F3
Milton *P. & K.*	12	B3
Milton Bridge	25	**E5**
Milton of Campsie	7	F1
Milton of Campsie	25	**E1**
Milton of Cullerlie	24	**A2**
Minard	11	E4
Minnigaff	2	B1
Mintlaw	17	F3
Moffat	8	B4
Mollinsburn	25	**F1**
Moniaive	7	G4
Monifieth	13	E3
Monifieth	24	**B4**
Monikie	24	**B4**
Monimail	13	D4
Monreith	2	B2
Montrose	13	E2
Moodiesburn	25	**E1**
Morar	10	C1
Morebattle	9	D3
Morenish	12	A3
Moresby	3	E3
Morningside	25	**E4**
Morpeth	4	C1
Moscow	7	F3
Mossat	17	D4
Mossblown	7	E3
Mossend	25	**F2**
Mosstodloch	16	C2
Motherwell	7	G2
Motherwell	25	**F3**
Mountbenger	8	C3
Moy	16	A3
Muchalls	13	F1
Muir of Fowlis	17	D4
Muir of Ord	15	F2
Muirdrum	13	E3
Muirdrum	24	**C4**
Muirhead *Angus*	13	D3
Muirhead *Angus*	24	**A4**
Muirhead *N.Lan.*	25	**E2**
Muirkirk	7	G3
Mulben	16	C2
Mundurno	24	**C1**
Munlochy	16	A2
Murroes	24	**B4**
Murton	5	D2
Musselburgh	8	C1
Musselburgh	25	**F4**
Muthill	12	B4
Mybster	19	E2
Myrebird	24	**A3**

N

Name	Pg	Ref
Nairn	16	A2
Nateby	4	B4
Near Sawrey	3	F4
Neilston	7	F2
Nenthead	4	B2
Nerston	25	**E3**
Netherley	13	F1
Netherley	24	**B3**
Netherton	9	E4
Nethy Bridge	16	B4
New Abbey	3	D1
New Aberdour	17	E2
New Byth	17	E2
New Cumnock	7	F4
New Deer	17	E3
New Galloway	2	C1
New Leeds	17	F2
New Luce	2	A1
New Pitsligo	17	E2
New Scone	12	C3
Newarthill	25	**F3**
Newbiggin-by-the-Sea	5	D1
Newbigging (East) *Angus*	24	**B4**
Newbigging (West) *Angus*	24	**B4**
Newbigging *S. Lan.*	8	A2
Newbridge	25	**D4**
Newburgh *Aber.*	17	F3
Newburgh *Fife*	13	D4
Newburn	4	C1
Newby Bridge	3	F4
Newcastle International Airport	4	C1
Newcastle upon Tyne	4	C1
Newcastleton	3	F1
Newcraighall	24	**F4**
Newhouse	25	**F2**
Newlandrig	25	**F5**
Newmachar	17	E4
Newmachar	24	**B1**
Newmains	8	A2
Newmarket	21	F2
Newmill	17	D2
Newmilns	7	F3
Newport	19	E3
Newport-on-Tay	13	D3
Newport-on-Tay	24	**B5**
Newton	11	E4
Newton Aycliffe	5	D3
Newton Mearns	7	F2
Newton Mearns	25	**D3**
Newton of Affleck	24	**B4**
Newton Stewart	2	B1
Newtongrange	25	**F5**
Newtonhill	13	F1
Newtonhill	24	**C3**
Newtonmore	16	A4
Newtown St. Boswells	9	D3
Newtyle	13	D3
Niddrie	25	**E4**
Nigg	24	**C2**
Ninemile Bar or Crocketford	3	D1
Nisbet	9	D3
Nitshill	25	**D2**
Norham	9	E2
North Ballachulish	11	E2
North Berwick	8	C1
North Cowton	5	D4
North Kessock	16	A3
North Middleton	8	C2
North Queensferry	8	B1
North Shields	5	D1
North Sunderland	9	F3
North Tarbothill	24	**C1**
Northallerton	5	D4
Northfield	24	**B2**
Norwick	23	F1

O

Name	Pg	Ref
Oakley	8	A1
Oban	11	D3
Ochiltree	7	F3
Ockle	10	C2
Oddsta	23	F1
Old Aberdeen	24	**C2**
Old Craighall	25	**F4**
Old Dailly	7	E4
Old Kinnernie	24	**A2**
Oldmeldrum	17	E3
Olgrinmore	19	E2
Ollaberry	23	E2
Onich	11	E2
Ormiston	8	C1
Orrok House	24	**C1**
Orton	4	A4
Oskaig	14	B3
Otter Ferry	6	D1
Otterburn	9	E4
Otterswick	23	F2
Overbister	22	C2
Overton *Aberdeen*	24	**B1**
Overton *Aber.*	24	**A1**
Overtown	8	A2
Oxnam	9	D3
Oxton	8	C2
Oykel Bridge	15	F1

P

Name	Pg	Ref
Paisley	7	F2
Palnackie	3	D2
Panbride	24	**C4**
Parkgate	3	E1
Partick	25	**D2**
Parton	3	D3
Path of Condie	12	C4
Pathhead	25	**F5**
Patna	7	E4
Patterdale	3	F3
Paxton	9	E2
Peebles	8	B3
Peel	2	B4
Pegswood	4	C1
Peinchorran	14	B3
Pencaitland	8	C1
Penicuik	8	B2
Penicuik	25	**E5**
Peninver	6	C3
Pennyghael	10	C3
Penpont	8	A4
Penrith	4	A3
Perth	12	C3
Peterculter	17	E4
Peterculter	24	**B2**
Peterhead	17	F3
Peterlee	5	D2
Pickering	5	F4
Pickletillem	24	**B5**
Pierowall	22	B2
Pinwherry	2	A1
Pinmill	6	C2
Pitagowan	12	B2
Pitlochry	12	B2
Pitmedden	17	E3
Pitscottie	13	D4
Pittenrail	16	A1
Pittenweem	13	E4
Plains	25	**F2**
Plean	8	A1
Polbeth	8	A2
Pollock	11	D2
Pollokshaws	25	**D2**
Polmont	8	A1
Polnoon	25	**D3**
Polton	25	**E5**
Polwarth	9	D2
Ponteland	4	C1
Poolewe	14	C1
Pooley Bridge	3	F3
Port Appin	11	D3
Port Askaig	6	B1
Port Bannatyne	7	D2
Port Driseach	6	D1
Port Ellen	6	A2
Port Elphinstone	24	**A1**
Port Glasgow	7	E1
Port Henderson	14	C2
Port Logan	2	A2
Port nan Giùran	21	F2
Port nan Long	20	B1
Port Nis	21	F1
Port of Menteith	12	A4
Port William	2	B2
Portencross	7	E2
Portknockie	17	D2
Portlethen	13	F1
Portlethen	24	**C3**
Portlethen Village	24	**C3**
Portmahomack	16	B1
Portnacon	18	B1
Portnacroish	11	D2
Portnahaven	6	A4
Portnalong	14	A3
Portobello	25	**F4**
Portpatrick	2	A2
Portree	14	B3
Portsoy	17	D2
Potterton	24	**C1**
Powburn	9	F3
Powmill	12	C4
Preston	9	D2
Prestonpans	8	C1
Prestonpans	25	**F4**
Prestwick	7	E3
Prestwick International Airport	7	E3
Prudhoe	4	C2

Q

Name	Pg	Ref
Quarter	25	**F3**

R

Name	Pg	Ref
Rafford	16	B2
Rait	13	D3
Ramsey	2	B4
Rathillet	13	D3
Rathillet	24	**A5**
Ratho	8	B1
Ratho	25	**D4**
Ratho Station	25	**D4**
Rattray	12	C3
Ravenglass	3	E4
Rawyards	25	**F2**

Name	Page	Grid
Reay	19	D1
Redcar	5	E3
Redcastle	15	F3
Redford	13	E3
Redhill	**24**	**A2**
Redpoint	14	C2
Reiss	19	F2
Renfrew	7	F1
Renfrew	**25**	**D2**
Rennington	9	F3
Rescobie	13	E2
Reston	9	E2
Rhiconich	18	B2
Rhu	7	E1
Rhynie	17	D3
Richmond	4	C4
Rickarton	13	F1
Riding Mill	4	C2
Riggend	**25**	**F2**
Rigside	8	A3
Ringford	2	C2
Roadside	19	E1
Roadside of Kinneff	13	F1
Roberton *Sc.Bord.*	8	C4
Roberton *S.Lan.*	8	A3
Robin Hood's Bay	5	F4
Rochester	9	E4
Rockcliffe	3	D2
Rogart	19	D4
Roghadal	21	D4
Romannobridge	8	B2
Rosedale Abbey	5	F4
Rosehearty	17	F2
Rosemarkie	16	A2
Rosewell	8	B2
Rosewell	**25**	**E5**
Roshven	11	D1
Roskhill	14	A3
Roslin	8	B2
Roslin	**25**	**E5**
Rothbury	9	E4
Rothes	16	C3
Rothesay	7	D2
Rothiesholm	22	C3
Rowlands Gill	4	C2
Roybridge	11	F1
Rutherend	**25**	**E3**
Rutherglen	7	F2
Rutherglen	**25**	**E2**
Ruthrieston	**24**	**C2**

S

Name	Page	Grid
Sacriston	4	C2
Saddell	6	C3
Saighdinis	20	B1
St. Abbs	9	E1
St. Andrews	13	E4
St. Bees	3	D3
St. Combs	17	F2
St. Cyrus	13	F2
St. Fergus	17	F2
St. Fillans	12	A3
St. John's Chapel	4	B2
St. John's Town of Dalry	2	C1
St. Margaret's Hope	22	B4
St. Mary's	22	B3
St. Monans	13	E4
Salen *Arg. & B.*	11	D2
Salen *High.*	11	D2
Saline	8	A1
Salmond's Muir	**24**	**C4**
Salsburgh	8	A2
Saltburn-by-the-Sea	5	E3
Saltcoats	7	E2
Sanaigmore	6	A3
Sandgarth	22	B3
Sandhead	2	A2
Sandness	23	D3
Sandsend	5	F3
Sandwick	23	E4
Sandygate	2	B4
Sanquhar	7	G4
Satley	4	C2
Scalasaig	10	B4
Scalby	5	F4
Scalloway	23	E3
Scapa	22	B3
Scarborough	5	F4
Scarinish	10	A3
Sconser	14	B3
Scorton	4	C4
Scotch Corner	4	C4
Scotton	4	C4
Scourie	18	A2
Scousburgh	23	E4
Scrabster	19	E1
Scremerston	9	E2
Seaham	5	D2
Seahouses	9	F3
Seamill	7	E2
Seascale	3	E4
Seaton	3	E3
Seaton Delaval	5	D1
Seaton Sluice	5	D1
Sedbergh	4	A4
Sedgefield	5	D3
Seghill	5	D1
Selkirk	8	C3
Sellafield	3	E4
Sellafirth	23	F1
Setter	23	E3
Sgiogarstaigh	21	F1
Shap	4	A3
Sherburn	5	D2
Shettleston	**25**	**E2**
Shiel Bridge	15	D4
Shieldaig	14	C2
Shilbottle	9	F4
Shildon	4	C3
Shinness Lodge	18	C3
Shiremoor	5	D1
Shotts	8	A2
Siabost	21	E1
Silloth	3	E2
Silverburn	**25**	**E5**
Siulaisiadar	21	F2
Skaill (East Coast) *Ork.*	22	C3
Skaill (West Coast) *Ork.*	22	A3
Skaw	23	F2
Skelmorlie	7	E1
Skelton	5	E3
Skelwick	22	B2
Skerray	18	C1
Skipness	6	C2
Slamannan	8	A1
Sleights	5	F4
Sligachan	14	B3
Smailholm	9	D3
Solas	20	B1
Sorbie	2	B2
Sorisdale	10	B2
Sorn	7	F3
South Bank	5	E3
South Hetton	5	D2
South Kirkton	**24**	**A2**
South Queensferry	8	B1
South Queensferry	**25**	**D4**
South Shields	5	D1
Southdean	9	D4
Southend	6	C4
Spean Bridge	11	F1
Spennymoor	5	D3
Spey Bay	16	C2
Spinningdale	16	A1
Spittal	19	E2
Spittal of Glenshee	12	C2
Springburn	**25**	**E2**
Springholm	3	D1
Springside	7	E3
Stadhlaigearraidh	20	A2
Staffin	14	B2
Staindrop	4	C3
Staintondale	5	F4
Stalling Busk	4	B4
Stamfordham	4	C1
Stand	**25**	**F2**
Stane	8	A2
Stanhope	4	B2
Stanley *Dur.*	4	C2
Stanley *P. & K.*	12	C3
Stannington	4	C1
Startforth	4	C3
Stenhousemuir	8	A1
Stenness	23	D2
Stenton	9	D1
Stepps	**25**	**E2**
Stevenston	7	E2
Stewarton	7	E2
Stichill	9	D3
Stirling	12	B4
Stobo	8	B3
Stocksfield	4	C2
Stockton-on-Tees	5	D3
Stoer	18	A3
Stokesley	5	E4
Stonefield	**25**	**E3**
Stonehaven	13	F1
Stonehouse	7	G2
Stoneykirk	2	A2
Stoneywood	**24**	**B1**
Stornoway	21	F2
Stow	8	C2
Strachan	13	E1
Strachur	11	E4
Straiton	**25**	**E5**
Straloch	12	C2
Stranraer	2	A2
Strathaven	7	G2
Strathblane	7	F1
Strathdon	16	C4
Strathmiglo	12	C4
Strathpeffer	15	F2
Strathy	19	D1
Strathyre	12	A4
Strichen	17	F2
Stromeferry	14	C3
Stromness	22	A3
Stronachlachar	11	F4
Strone	7	E1
Strontian	11	D2
Stuartfield	17	F3
Sumburgh	23	E4
Sunderland	5	D2
Sunnyside	**24**	**B3**
Swinton	9	E2
Symbister	23	F2
Symington *S.Ayr.*	7	E3
Symington *S.Lan.*	8	A3
Syre	18	C2

T

Name	Page	Grid
Tabost	21	F1
Tain	16	A1
Talisker	14	A3
Talladale	15	D2
Tannadice	13	E2
Tannochside	**25**	**F2**
Taobh Tuath	21	D3
Tarbert (Jura) *Arg. & B.*	6	B1
Tarbert (Kintyre) *Arg. & B.*	6	C1
Tarbet	11	F4
Tarbolton	7	F3
Tarfside	13	E1
Tarrel	16	B1
Tarves	17	E3
Tavelty	**24**	**A1**
Tayinloan	6	C2
Taynuilt	11	E3
Tayport	13	D3
Tayport	**24**	**B5**
Tayvallich	6	C1
Teangue	14	C4
Tebay	4	A4
Teesside International Airport	5	D3
Temple Sowerby	4	A3
Teviothead	8	C4
Thainstone House	**24**	**A1**
The Birks	**24**	**A2**
The Neuk	**24**	**A3**
Thornaby-on-Tees	5	D3
Thornhill *D. & G.*	8	A4
Thornhill *Stir.*	12	A4
Thornley	5	D2
Thornliebank	**25**	**D3**
Thornton	13	D4
Thorntonhall	**25**	**D3**
Threlkeld	3	F3
Thriepley	**24**	**A4**
Thropton	9	E4
Thrumster	19	F2
Thursby	3	F2
Thurso	19	E1
Thwaite	4	B4
Tibbermore	12	C3
Tighnabruaich	6	D1
Tillicoultry	12	B4
Tillyfourie	17	D4
Timsgearraidh	21	D2
Tingwall	22	B3
Toab	23	E4
Tobermory	10	C2
Toberonochy	11	D4
Todhills	**24**	**B4**
Toft	23	E2
Togston	9	F4
Tolastadh a'Chaolais	21	E2
Tolastadh Ùr	21	F1
Toll of Birness	17	F3
Tollcross	**25**	**E2**
Tomatin	16	A3
Tomich	16	A2
Tomintoul	16	C4
Tomnavoulin	16	C3
Tongland	2	C2
Tongue	18	C2
Tore	15	F2
Tormore	6	C3
Torphichen	8	A1
Torphins	17	D4
Torrance *E.Dun.*	7	F1
Torrance *E.Dun.*	**25**	**E2**
Torrance *S.Lan.*	**25**	**E3**
Torridon	15	D2
Torrin	14	B4
Torry	**24**	**C2**
Torthorwald	3	E1
Torver	3	F4
Toscaig	14	C3
Tow Law	4	C2
Town Yetholm	9	E3
Townhead of Greenlaw	3	D1
Tranent	8	C1
Tressait	12	B2
Trimdon	5	D3
Trinity	13	E2
Trochry	12	C3
Troon	7	E3
Troutbeck	3	F4
Troutbeck Bridge	3	F4
Tummel Bridge	12	B2
Tunga	21	F2
Turnberry	7	E4
Turriff	17	E2
Twatt	22	A2
Twechar	7	G1
Twechar	**25**	**E1**
Tweedmouth	9	E2
Tweedsmuir	8	B3
Twynholm	2	C2
Tyndrum	11	F3
Tynemouth	5	D1

U

Name	Page	Grid
Uachdar	20	B2
Uddingston	7	G2
Uddingston	**25**	**E2**
Uddington	8	A3
Uig	14	B2
Ulbster	19	F2
Ulgham	9	F4
Ullapool	15	D1
Ulpha	3	E4
Ulsta	23	E2
Unapool	18	B2
Upper Burnhaugh	**24**	**B3**
Upper Knockando	16	C3
Upper Muirskie	**24**	**B3**
Upper Victoria	**24**	**C4**
Urafirth	23	E2
Ushaw Moor	4	C2
Uyeasound	23	F1

V

Name	Page	Grid
Valsgarth	23	F1
Veensgarth	23	E3
Vidlin	23	F2
Viewpark	**25**	**F2**
Voe	23	E2

W

Name	Page	Grid
Walls	23	E3
Wallsend	5	D1
Wallyford	**25**	**F4**
Warcop	4	A3
Wark	4	B1
Warkworth	9	F4
Warwick Bridge	3	F2
Wasbister	22	B2
Washington	5	D2
Watchgate	4	A4
Waterbeck	3	F1
Waterfoot	**25**	**D3**
Waterside	**25**	**E1**
Watten	19	F2
Wattston	**25**	**F2**
Weem	12	B2
Wellbank	**24**	**B4**
Wemyss Bay	7	E1
Wensley	4	C4
West Auckland	4	C3
West Calder	8	A2
West Kilbride	7	E2
West Linton	8	B2
West Park	**24**	**A3**
West Tarbert	6	C1
West Yell	23	E2
Wester Fintray	**24**	**B1**
Wester Ord	**24**	**B2**
Westerdale	19	E2
Westerton	**24**	**A3**
Westgate	4	B2
Westhill	17	E4
Westhill	**24**	**B2**
Westness	22	B2
Westnewton	3	E2
Westruther	9	D2
Westside	**24**	**B3**
Wetheral	3	F2
Whalton	4	C1
Whauphill	2	B2
Wheatley Hill	5	D2
Whickham	4	C2
Whifflet	**25**	**F2**
Whitburn	8	A2
Whitby	5	F3
Whitecairns	**24**	**C1**
Whitecraig	8	C1
Whitecraig	**25**	**F4**
Whitehall	22	C2
Whitehaven	3	D3
Whitehills	17	E2
Whiterashes	17	E4
Whithorn	2	B2
Whiting Bay	6	D3
Whitley Bay	5	D1
Whittingham	9	E4
Wick	19	F2
Wigton	3	F2
Wigtown	2	B2
Wilkieston	**25**	**D5**
Willington	4	C3
Winchburgh	8	B1
Windermere	3	F4
Windygates	13	D4
Wingate	5	D2
Winston	4	C3
Winton	4	B3
Wishaw	8	A2
Wishaw	**25**	**F3**
Witton Gilbert	4	C2
Wolsingham	4	C2
Woodhaven	**24**	**B5**
Woodland	4	C3
Woodside	**24**	**C2**
Wooler	9	E3
Workington	3	E3
Wormit	13	D3
Wormit	**24**	**A5**
Wrelton	5	F4

Y

Name	Page	Grid
Yarm	5	D3
Yarrow	8	C3
Yetts o' Muckhart	12	C4
Yoker	**25**	**D2**

Abbreviations used in town plan indexes

All	Alley
App	Approach
Arc	Arcade
Av	Avenue
Bk	Bank
Bldgs	Buildings
Boul	Boulevard
Bri	Bridge
Cen	Central/Centre
Cft	Croft
Ch	Church
Circ	Circus
Clo	Close
Coll	College
Cor	Corner
Cotts	Cottages
Cres	Crescent
Ct	Court
Dr	Drive
E	East
Esp	Esplanade
Est	Estate
Ex	Exchange
Fm	Farm
Gdn	Garden
Gdns	Gardens
Gra	Grange
Grn	Green
Gro	Grove
Hts	Heights
Ho	House
Hos	Hospital
Ind	Industrial
Junct	Junction
La	Lane
Ln	Loan
Mans	Mansion
Mkt	Market
Ms	Mews
Mt	Mount
N	North
Par	Parade
Pk	Park
Pl	Place
Quad	Quadrant
Rd	Road
Ri	Rise
S	South
Sch	School
Sq	Square
St	Street
St.	Saint
Sta	Station
Ter	Terrace
Twr	Tower
Vills	Villas
Vw	View
W	West
Wd	Wood
Wds	Woods
Wf	Wharf
Wk	Walk
Wks	Works
Yd	Yard

The indexes contain streets that are not named on the map due to insufficient space. For each of these cases the nearest street that does appear on the map is also listed in *italics*.

KEY TO MAP SYMBOLS

Symbol	Meaning
M74	Motorway
A82	Primary road dual / single
A70	'A' Road dual / single
B793	'B' Road dual / single
	Other road dual / single
Toll →	One-way street / Toll
	Restricted access / Pedestrian street
	Minor road / Track
FB	Footpath / Cycle path / Footbridge
	Railway line / station
	Railway tunnel / Level crossing
	Bus / Coach station
P	Car Park
	Leisure / Tourism
	Shopping / Retail
	Administration / Law
	Education
	Hospital
	Industry / Commerce
	Notable building
	Health centre
Pol PO Lib	Police station / Post Office / Library
+ ☾ ✡	Church / Mosque / Synagogue
🎥 🎭	Cinema / Theatre
⊠ Hilton	Major Hotel
i i	Tourist information centre (all year / seasonal)
	Fire station / Ambulance station / Community centre

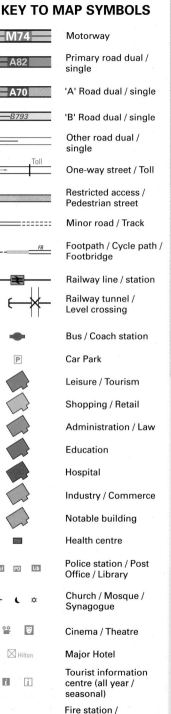

Maps 32-35   **Index 36-37**
Scale 4 inches to 1 mile

ABERDEEN

Maps 38-39   **Index 40-41**
Scale 4.6 inches to 1 mile

DUNDEE

Maps 42-51   **Index 52-57**
Scale 4 inches to 1 mile
City centre map 5.7 miles to 1 inch

EDINBURGH

Maps 58-65   **Index 66-72**
Scale 4 inches to 1 mile

GLASGOW

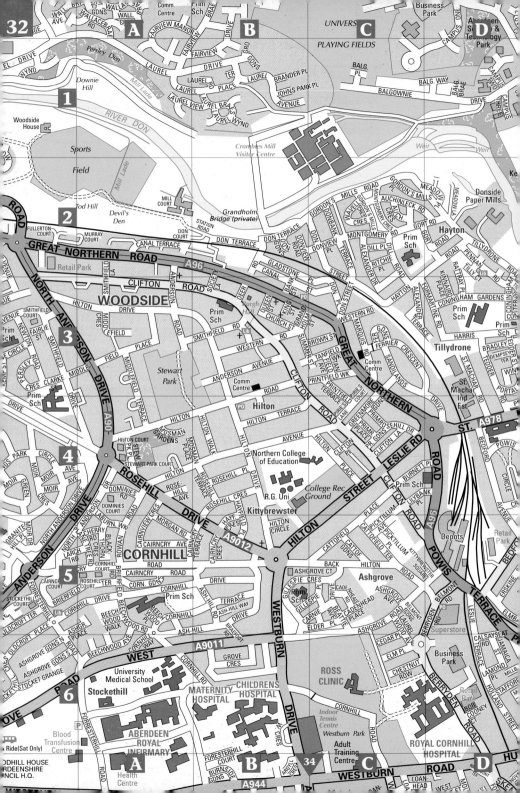

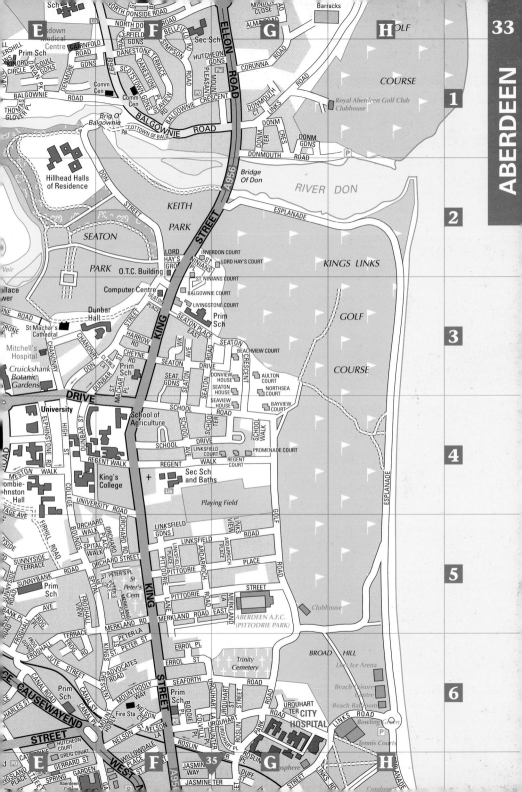

INDEX TO STREETS

A
Abbey La 35H4
Abbey Pl 35H4
Abbey Rd 35H4
Abbey Sq 35H4
Abbotsford La 35E4
Abbotsford Pl 35E4
  Ferryhill Rd
Aberdeen Mkt 35F2
  Union St
Aberdon Ct 32D3
  Coningham Ter
Aberdon Ho Ct 32D3
  Coningham Rd
Abergeldie Rd 34C5
Abergeldie Ter 34C5
Academy St 35E3
Adelphi 35F2
Adelphi La 35F2
  Adelphi
Advocates Rd 33F6
Affleck Pl 35E3
  Marywell St
Affleck St 35E3
Albert La 34B3
Albert Pl 34C2
Albert Quay 35G3
Albert St 34C3
Albert Ter 34C3
Albert Wk 34C3
  Albert Ter
Albury Gdns 35E4
  Albury Rd
Albury Mans 35E4
  Albury Rd
Albury Pl 35E4
Albury Rd 34D4
Albyn Gro 34C3
Albyn La 34C3
Albyn Pl 34C3
Albyn Ter 34C3
Alexander Dr 32C2
Alexander Ter 32C3
Alford La 34D3
Alford Pl 34D3
  Albyn Pl
Allan St 34C4
Allenvale Gdns 34D6
Allenvale Rd 34D6
Anderson Av 32B3
Anderson Rd 32A2
Ann St 34D1
Annfield Ter 34B4
Ardarroch Cl 33G5
  Ardarroch Rd
Ardarroch Pl 33G5
Ardarroch Rd 33F5
Argyll Cres 34B1
Argyll Pl 34B1
Ash-hill Dr 32A5
Ash-hill Pl 32B5
  Spital
Ash-hill Rd 32B5
Ash-hill Way 32B5
Ashgrove Av 32C5
Ashgrove Ct 32B5
Ashgrove Rd 32C5
Ashley Gdns 34B4
Ashley Gro 34C4
Ashley La 34B4
Ashley Pk Dr 34B4
Ashley Pk La 34C4
Ashley Pk N 34B4
Ashley Pk S 34C4
Ashley Rd 34C4
Ashvale Ct 34D3
  Cuparstone Row
Ashvale Pl 34C3
Auchinleck Cres 32C2
Auchinleck Rd 32C2
Auchlossan Ct 33E1
  Davan Pk
Auckland Pl 33F5
  Merkland Pl
Aulton Ct 33G3

B
Back Hilton Rd 32C5
Back Wynd 35E2
Baker Pl 34D1
  Baker St
Baker St 34D1
Balgownie Brae 32D1
Balgownie Ct 33F3
Balgownie Cres 33F1
Balgownie Dr 32C1
Balgownie Gdns 32D1
Balgownie Pl 32C1
Balgownie Rd 33F1
Balgownie Way 32C1
Balmoral Ct 34C5
Balmoral Pl 34C5
Balmoral Rd 34D5
Balmoral Ter 34C5
Balnagask Wk 35H5
  Farquhar Rd
Baltic Pl 35H2
Baltic St 35G2
Bank St 35E4
Bank St 32B3
  (Woodside)

Bannermill Pl 35G1
  Beach Boul
Bannermill St 35G1
  Cotton St
Barkmill Rd 32C5
  Ashgrove Rd
Barron St 32C3
  Sandilands Dr
Bath St 35E2
  Windmill Brae
Battock Pl 35G5
Baxter St 35H4
Bayview Ct 33G4
Bayview Rd 34A3
Bayview Rd S 34A4
Beach Boul 35G1
Beachview Ct 33G3
Beaconsfield Pl 34A3
Beattie Av 32C5
Beattie Pl 32C5
  Elder Pl
Bedford Av 32D4
Bedford Pl 32D5
Bedford Rd 32D5
Beechgrove Av 34B2
Beechgrove Ct 34B2
  Beechgrove Ter
Beechgrove Gdns 34B1
Beechgrove Pl 34B2
Beechgrove Ter 34B2
Beechwood Av 32A6
Beechwood Ct 32A5
Beechwood Rd 32A5
Beechwood Wk 32A5
Belgrave Ter 34C2
Belmont Gdns 32C5
Belmont Rd 32D5
Belmont St 35E2
Belvidere Cres 34C2
Belvidere St 34C1
Berry St 35F1
Berryden 32D6
  Business Pk
  Berryden Rd
Berryden Rd 32D6
Bethany Gdns 34D4
Birch Rd 32A5
  Rowan Rd
Blackburn Pl 33E4
  High St
Blackfriars St 35E1
Blacks La 35G3
Blackthorn Cres 32A5
Blaikies Quay 35G2
Blenheim La 34B2
Blenheim Pl 34B2
Bloomfield Ct 34D5
Bloomfield Pl 34D4
Bloomfield Rd 34D5
Boa Vista Pl 33E5
Bob Cooney Ct 32D6
Boddie Pl 33F6
Bon Accord Cres 35E3
Bon Accord Cres 35E3
  Bon Accord Cres
Bon Accord La 35E3
Bon Accord Sq 35E3
Bon Accord St 35E3
Bon Accord Ter 34D3
Bonnymuir Pl 34B1
Bradley Ter 32D3
Braefoot Rd 32B5
Braemar Pl 34C5
Brander Pl 32B1
Brebner's Ct 35F1
  Justice St
Brewery La 33E4
  High St
Bridge of Don 33G2
Bridge Pl 35E2
  Bridge St
Bridge St 35E2
Bridge St 32A2
  (Woodside)
  Great Northern Rd
Brierfield Rd 32A5
Brig o' Balgownie 33F1
Bright St 35E5
Brighton Pl 34B4
Brimmond Pl 34C5
Broad St 35F2
Broomhill Av 34C6
Broomhill Pk 34C5
  Broomhill Rd
Broomhill Pl 34C6
Broomhill Rd 34C5
Broomhill Ter 34C6
Brough Pl 32B5
  Carnie Dr
Brown St 32C3
Brunswick St 35E5
Burnbank Pl 35H5
Burnbank Ter 35H5
Burnett Pl 32C4
Burns Gdns 34A4
Burns Rd 34A4
Burnside Gdns 34B1

C
Cadenhead Pl 32C5
Cadenhead Rd 32C5

Cairnaquheen 34A1
  Gdns
Cairnaquheen Pl 34A2
  Cairnaquheen
  Gdns
Cairncry Av 32A5
Cairncry Cres 32B5
Cairncry Rd 32A5
Cairncry Ter 32A5
Cairnfield Pl 34B1
Cairnfield Rd 33E1
Cairnview Cres 32A5
Caledonian Brae 35E4
  Ferryhill Rd
Caledonian Ct 35H4
  Ferryhill Rd
Caledonian La 35E4
  Caledonian Pl
Caledonian Pl 35E4
Calsayseat Rd 32D6
Camperdown Rd 34A1
Campus One 32D1
Campus Three 32D1
Campus Two 32D1
Canal Pl 33E6
Canal Rd 33E6
Canal St 33E6
Canal St 32B2
  (Woodside)
Canal Ter 32A2
Candlemakers La 35E1
  Loch St
Carden Pl 34B3
Carden Ter 34C3
Carlton Pl 34A2
Carmelite La 35F2
  Wapping St
Carmelite St 35F2
  Wapping St
Carnegies Brae 35F2
  Flourmill La
Carnie Dr 32B5
Carnie Gdns 32B5
  Carnie Dr
Caroline 34D1
  Apartments
  Forbes St
Caroline Pl 34D1
  Hutcheon St
Castle St 35F2
Castle Ter 35G2
Castlegate 35F2
Castlehill 35G1
  Hanover St
Catherine St 35E1
Cattofield Gdns 32C5
Cattofield Pl 32C5
Cattofield Ter 32C5
Causewayend 33E6
Cedar Pl 32C6
Chanonry 33E3
Chapel Ct 35G2
  Justice St
Chapel St 34D2
Charles St 33E6
  Charles St
Charlotte Gdns 35E1
Charlotte Pl 35E1
Charlotte St 35E1
Chattan Pl 34C4
Cherry Rd 32A5
Chestnut Row 32C6
Cheyne Rd 33F3
Church St 35G2
Church St 32B3
  (Woodside)
Church Wk 33E4
  High St
Claremont Gdns 34C4
Claremont Gro 34C4
Claremont Pl 34C4
Claremont St 34C4
Clarence St 35G2
Clarks La 33F3
Clifton Ct 32C3
  Great Northern Rd
Clifton La 32C4
Clifton Pl 32C4
Clifton Rd 32A3
Clyde St 35G3
College Bounds 33E4
College St 35E3
Colville Pl 33E4
Commerce St 35G2
Commercial Quay 35G3
Concert Ct 35E2
  Broad St
Coningham Gdns 32D3
Coningham Rd 32D3
Coningham Ter 32D3
Constitution Ct 35G1
  Constitution St
Constitution La 35G1
  Wales St
Constitution St 35G1
Cornhill Ct 32A5
Cornhill Dr 32A6
Cornhill Rd 32A6
Cornhill Sq 32B5
  Ash-hill Rd

Cornhill Ter 32A5
Cornhill Way 32A6
Correction Wynd 35F2
  Schoolhill
Corsehill Gdns 32D1
Corunna Rd 33G1
Cottage Brae 34C4
Cotton St 35G1
Cottown of 33F1
  Balgownie
Coull Gdns 33E1
Cowan Pl 32C2
  Alexander Dr
Craibstone La 35E4
  Bon Accord St
Craig Pl 35F4
  Menzies Rd
Craigie Loanings 34C2
Craigie Pk 34C2
Craigie Pk Pl 34C2
Craigie St 35E1
Craigielea Av 34A5
Craigton Ct 34A6
Cranford Pl 34B6
Cranford Rd 34C6
Cranford St 34B6
Crathie Gdns W 34D6
Crathie Ter 34C6
Crimon Pl 35E2
Crombie Pl 35G4
Crombie Rd 35G4
Cromwell Ct 34B4
  Forbesfield Rd
Cromwell Gdns 34A4
Cromwell Rd 34A4
Crooked La 35E1
Crown La 35E3
  Crown Ter
Crown St 35E3
Crown Ter 35E3
Cuparstone Ct 35E3
  Cuparstone Row
Cuparstone La 34D3
  Cuparstone Row
Cuparstone Row 34D3

D
Danestone Pl 33F1
Danestone Ter 33F1
Davan Pk 33E1
Dee Pl 35E3
Dee St 35E3
Deemount Av 35E5
Deemount Gdns 35E5
Deemount Rd 35E5
Deer Rd 32B3
Dempsey Ter 32D3
Denburn Ct 35E1
Denburn Rd 35E1
  Gilcomston Pk
Denmore Gdns 33E1
Denmore Rd 33E1
Desswood Pl 34B3
Devanha Cres 35E4
Devanha Gdns 35E4
Devanha Gdns E 35E4
Devanha Gdns S 35E5
Devanha Gdns W 35E5
Devanha Ter 35E4
  Devanha Gdns
Devonshire Rd 34B4
Diamond La 35E2
  Diamond St
Diamond Pl 35E2
  Union St
Diamond St 35E2
Dill Pl 32C2
Dill Rd 32C2
Dock St E 35H3
  Blaikies Quay
Dock St W 35H3
  Blaikies Quay
Dominies Ct 32A4
Dominies Rd 32A4
Don Ct 32A2
Don Gdns 32B2
Don Pl 32C3
Don St 32E3
  (Old Aberdeen)
Don St (Woodside) 32A4
Don Ter 32B2
Donald Pl 34D1
Donbank Ter 32C2
Donmouth Ct 33G1
Donmouth Cres 33G1
Donmouth Gdns 33G1
Donmouth Rd 33G1
Donmouth Ter 33G1
Donside Ct 32C2
  Auchinleck Rd
Donview Ho 33G3
Donview Pl 32C2
Donview Rd 32B2
Douglas La 33E4
  High St
Downies Brae 35G5
Downies Pl 35H5
Duff St 35G1
Dunbar St 33E4

Duncans Pl 33E4
  High St
Duthie Ct 34A5
  Duthie Ter
Duthie Pl 34A6
Duthie Ter 34A6

E
East Craibstone St 35E4
  Bon Accord St
East Grn 35F2
  Market St
East N St 35F1
East Tullos Ind Est 35H6
Eden Pl 34D1
Elder Pl 32B5
Elm Pl 32C6
Elmbank Rd 33E6
Elmbank Ter 32D5
Elmfield Av 32D5
Elmfield Pl 32D5
Elphinstone Ct 32C2
  Auchinleck Cres
Elphinstone Rd 33E4
Errol Pl 33F6
Errol St 33F6
Erskine St 32D5
Esplanade 35H2
Esslemont Av 34C1
Exchange La 35F2
  Exchange St
Exchange St 35F2
Exchequer Row 35F2
  Shiprow

F
Fairview Brae 32A1
Fairview Dr 32B1
Farmers Hall La 34D1
Farquhar Av 35H5
Farquhar Brae 35H5
Farquhar Rd 35H5
Farrier La 35F1
  Mealmarket St
Fernie Brae 35G6
Ferrier Cres 32C3
Ferrier Gdns 32C3
Ferry Pl 35H3
Ferryhill Gdns 35E4
Ferryhill La 35E4
Ferryhill Pl 35E4
Ferryhill Rd 35E4
Ferryhill Ter 35E4
Firhill Pl 33E5
Firhill Rd 33E5
  Spital Wk
Fish St 35G2
Flourmill La 35F2
Fonthill Gdns E 34D5
Fonthill Gdns W 34D4
Fonthill Rd 34D4
Fonthill Ter 34D4
Forbes St 34D1
Forbesfield La 34B4
Forbesfield Rd 34B4
Forest Av 34B4
Forest Av La 34B4
Forest Rd 34B4
Foresterhill Ct 34B4
Forestgait 34A2
Formartine Rd 32C3
Forresterhill Rd 32A6
Fountainhall Rd 34B2
Fountville Ct 32B3
  Summer St
Fowlershill Gdns 33E1
Fraser Ct 33E6
Fraser Pl 32D6
Fraser Rd 32D6
Fraser St 32D6
Frederick St 35F1
Freefield Gdns 33F1
Friendship Ter 34C4
  Ashley Rd
Froghall Av 33E6
Froghall Gdns 33E6
Froghall Pl 33E5
Froghall Rd 33E6
Froghall Ter 33E6
Froghall Vw 33E5

G
Gaelic La 35E2
Gairn Circle 34D5
Gairn Ct 34D5
  Belmont St
Gairn Cres 34D5
Gairn Rd 34D5
Gairn Ter 34D5
Gallowgate 35F1
Garvock Wynd 35G2
George St 33E6
Gerrard St 35E1
Gilcomston Ct 34D2
  Kidd St
Gilcomston Land 34D2
  Kidd St
Gilcomston Pk 34D2
Gilcomston Steps 34D1
Gilcomston Ter 34D1
  Farmers Hall La

Gillespie Cres 32B5
Gillespie Pl 32B5
Girdleness Rd 35H5
Girdleness Ter 35G6
Girdlestone Pl 35H5
Gladstone Pl 34B3
Gladstone Pl 32B2
  (Woodside)
Glenbervie Rd 35G4
Glendale Ms 34D3
  Union Glen
Golden Sq 35E2
Golf Rd 33G5
Gordon La 34A6
Gordon St 35E3
Gordondale Ct 34A2
Gordondale Rd 34B1
Gordon's Mills 32C2
  Cres
Gordon's Mills Pl 32C2
Gordon's Mills Rd 32C2
Gort Rd 32C2
Gort Ter 32C2
  Auchinleck Rd
Grampian La 35G4
Grampian Pl 35F5
Grampian Rd 35G5
Grandholm Br 32B2
Grandholm Br 32B2
  (Private)
Grandholm Ct 32C2
  Montgomery Rd
Grandholm St 32B3
Granton St 34C3
Grants Pl 33E4
  High St
Granville Pl 34B5
Gray St 34B5
Gray St Ms 34B5
Great Northern Rd 32C3
Great Southern Rd 34D5
Great Western Pl 34C4
Great Western Rd 34A5
Green, The 35F2
  Rennies Wynd
Greenmore Gdns 32C4
Greenwell Pl 35H6
Greenwell Rd 35H6
Gregness Gdns 35H6
Greig Ct 35E1
Grosvenor Pl 34C2
Grosvenor Ter 34D2
  Grosvenor Pl
Grove Cres 32B6
Guestrow 35F2
  Broad St
Guild St 35F3

H
Hadden St 35F2
Hamilton La 34A2
  Hamilton Pl
Hamilton Pl 34A2
Hammerfield Av 34A5
Hammersmith Rd 34B5
Hanover St 35G1
Harcourt Rd 34A1
Hardgate 34D4
Hardgate La 34D5
  Hardgate
Harlaw Pl 34A4
Harlaw Rd 34A4
Harlaw Ter 34A4
Harriet St 35E2
Harris Dr 32D3
Harrow Rd 33F3
Hartington Rd 34B3
Hawthorn Ter 33G6
Hayfield Cres 32B5
Hayfield Pl 32B4
Hayton Rd 32C3
Hermitage Av 33E4
High St 35F5
Highgate Gdns 35F5
Hill St 34D1
Hill Vw Gdns 35G6
Hillhead Ter 33E5
  Spital
Hillview Rd 35G6
Hilton Av 32A4
Hilton Circle 32B5
Hilton Ct 32A4
Hilton Dr 32B4
Hilton Pl 32C4
Hilton Rd 32B5
Hilton St 32B5
Hilton Ter 32B4
Hilton Wk 32B4
Holburn Pl 34C5
Holburn St 34C4
Holland Pl 32D6
Holland St 32D6
Hollybank Pl 34D4
Hosefield Av 34B1
Hosefield Rd 34B1
Howburn Pl 34D4
Hunter Pl 33F6
Huntly St 34D2
Hutcheon Ct 33E1
Hutcheon Gdns 33E1

Hutcheon St 34D1
Hutchison Ter 34A6

I
Imperial Pl 35 F2
  Guild St
Inverdon Ct 33 F2
Irvine Pl 34 C5

J
Jacks Brae 34D2
Jackson Ter 33 F6
  Urquhart La
Jamaica St 32D6
James St 35G2
Jamiesons Quay 35 F3
Jasmine Pl 35 F1
Jasmine Way 35 F1
Jasmine Ter 35 F1
John St 35 E1
Johns Pk Pl 32 B1
Jopps La 35 E1
Justice Mill Brae 34D3
  Justice Mill La
Justice Mill La 34D3
Justice Port 35G1
  Beach Boul
Justice St 35 F2
Jute St 33 E6

K
Kerloch Gdns 35 F5
Kerloch Pl 35 F5
Kettocks Mill Rd 33 E2
Kidd St 34D2
King George VI Br 35 E6
King St 33 F3
King St 32 B3
  (Woodside)
King's Ct 32 C2
  Auchinleck Rd
Kings Cres 33 F6
King's Gate 34A2
Kings Rd 32 C2
  Auchinleck Rd
Kingsland Pl 35 E1
Kinnaird Pl 32D2
Kinord Circle 33 E1
Kintore Gdns 34D1
  Kintore Pl
Kintore Pl 34D1
Kirkhill Pl 35H6
Kirkhill Rd 35G6
Kittybrewster Sq 32 C5

L
Laburnam Wk 32A5
Ladywell Pl 35H5
Lamond Pl 32D6
Langstane Pl 35 E3
Laurel Av 32 B1
Laurel Braes 32 B1
Laurel Dr 32A1
Laurel Gdns 32 B1
Laurel Gro 32 B1
Laurel La 32 B1
  Laurel Dr
Laurel Pk 32 B1
  Laurel Braes
Laurel Pl 32A1
Laurel Rd 32A1
Laurel Ter 32 B1
Laurel Vw 32A1
Laurel Wynd 32 B1
Laurelwood Av 32 C5
Leadside Rd 34D2
Learney Pl 34A4
Lemon Pl 35G1
  Park St
Lemon St 35G1
Leslie Rd 32 C4
Leslie Ter 32D5
Lilybank Pl 32 C4
Lime St 35H2
Lindsay St 35 E2
  Golden Sq
Links Pl 35H2
Links Rd 35H1
Links Rd 33G1
  (Br.Don)
Links St 35H2
Links Vw 33G5
Linksfield Ct 33G4
Linksfield Gdns 33 F5
Linksfield Pl 33 F5
Linksfield Rd 33 F5
Little Belmont St 35 E2
  Belmont St
Little Chapel St 34D2
  Chapel St
Littlejohn St 35 F1
Livingstone Ct 33 F3
Loanhead Pl 34 C1
Loanhead Ter 34 C1
Loanhead Wk 34 C1
Loch St 35 F1
Lodge Wk 35 F2
  Union St
Loirston Pl 35H5
Lord Hay's Ct 35G2
Lord Hay's Gro 33 F2
Louisville Av 34A4

M
Maberly St 35 E1
Mackenzie Pl 33 E4
  High St
Mackie Pl 34D2
Magdala Pl 34D1
  Short Loanings
Maitlands Quay 35H4
  Sinclair Rd
Mansefield Pl 35H5
Mansefield Rd 35H4
Margaret Pl 34 C6
Margaret St 34D2
  Rose St
Marine Ct 35 E4
  Marine Ter
Marine La 35 E4
  Abbotsford La
Marine Ter 35 E4
  South Crown St
Marine Ter 35 E4
Marischal Ct 35 F2
  Justice St
Marischal St 35 F2
Market La 33 E4
Market St 35 F2
Marquis Rd 32 C3
Martins La 35 F2
  Rennies Wynd
Marywell St 35 F3
Matthews Quay 35H3
May Baird Av 32 C5
  Ashgrove Rd
Mayfield Gdns 34A4
McCombies Ct 34D3
  Union St
Meadow Ct 32 C2
  Gordon's Mills Cres
Meadow La 32D2
Meadow St 32 C2
Mealmarket St 35 F1
Menzies Rd 35G4
Merkland La 33G5
Merkland Pl 33 F5
Merkland Rd 33 F5
Merkland Rd E 33 F5
Meston Wk 33 E4
Midchingle Rd 35G3
Middlefield Cres 32A3
Middlefield Ter 32A3
Middlefield Wk 32A4
  Hilton Rd
Mile-End Av 34 B1
Mile-End La 34 B1
Mile-End Pl 34 B1
Mill Ct 32A2
Millbank La 32D6
Millbank Pl 32D6
Millburn St 35 E4
Miller St 35G2
Minister La 34D2
  Summer St
Montgomery Cres 32 C2
Montgomery Rd 32 C2
Morgan Rd 32A5
Morningside Gdns 34A6
Morningside Gro 34A6
  Morningside Rd
Morningside La 34A6
Morningside Pl 34A6
Morningside Rd 34A6
Morningside Ter 34A6
Morven Pl 35G5
Mosman Gdns 32A4
Mosman Pl 32A4
Mount Pleasant 33G1
Mount St 34D1
Mounthooly 33 F6
Mounthooly Way 33 F6
Mountview Gdns 34D1
  Mount St
Murray Ct 32A2
Murray Ter 35 E5

N
Nellfield Pl 34 C4
Nelson Ct 33 F6
Nelson La 33 F6
Nelson St 33 F6
Netherkirkgate 35 F2
  Union St
Newlands Av 34 B6
Newlands Cres 34 B6
Norfolk Rd 34 B5
North Esplanade E 35G3
North Esplanade W 35 F4
North Grampian 35G5
  Circle
North St. Andrew 35 E1
  St
  St. Andrew St
North Silver St 35 E3
Northfield Pl 34D2
Northsea Ct 33G3
Novar Pl 34D1

O
Oakhill Cres 34A2
Oakhill Rd 34A2

Old Ch Rd 35G6
Old Ford Rd 35 F4
Oldmill Rd 35 E4
  Bon Accord St
Orchard, The 33 E5
Orchard La 33 F5
  Orchard Pl
Orchard Pl 33 E5
Orchard Rd 33 F5
Orchard St 33 E5
Orchard Wk 33 E5
Osborne Pl 34 B2
Oscar Pl 35G5
Oscar Rd 35G5

P
Palmerston Pl 35 F4
Palmerston Rd 35 F4
Park La 35G1
  Princes St
Park Pl 35 F1
  Park St
Park Rd 33G6
Park St 35G1
Patagonian Ct 35 E4
  Belmont St
Peacocks Cl 35 F1
  East N St
Pennan Rd 32D2
Picardy Ct 34D3
Picktillum Av 32 C5
Picktillum St 32 C5
Pirie's Ct 32 C4
Pirie's La 32 C4
Pitstruan Pl 34 C4
Pitstruan Ter 34 C5
Pittodrie La 33 F5
Pittodrie Pl 33 F5
Pittodrie St 33 F5
Polmuir Av 35 E5
Polmuir Pl 35 E5
Polmuir Rd 35 E5
Polwarth Rd 35 F5
Portal Cres 32D3
Portal Ter 32D4
Porthill Ct 35 F1
  Gallowgate
Portland St 35 F4
Poultry Mkt La 35 F2
  Queen St
Powis Circle 32D4
Powis Cres 32D4
Powis La 33 E6
Powis Pl 32D6
Powis Ter 32D5
Poynernook Rd 35 F3
Primrosehill Dr 32 C4
Primrosehill Gdns 32 C4
Primrosehill Pl 32 C4
Prince Arthur St 34 C2
Princes St 35 F1
Printfield Ter 32 C3
Printfield Wk 32 C3
Promenade Ct 33G4
Prospect Ct 35 F4
Prospect Ter 35 F4

Q
Queen Elizabeth II 35 F4
  Br
Queen St 35 F2
Queen St 32 B3
  (Woodside)
Queens Ct 34A4
Queen's Cross 34 B3
Queens Gdns 34 B3
Queen's Gate 34A3
Queens La N 34 B3
Queens La S 34A3
Queens Links 35H1
  Leisure Pk
Queens Ter 34 C3

R
Raeburn Pl 35 E1
Raeden Av 34A1
Raeden Pk Rd 34A1
Raik Rd 35 F3
Rattray Pl 32D2
Regent Ct 33G4
Regent Quay 35G2
Regent Rd 35G3
Regent Wk 33 F4
Rennies Wynd 35 F2
Richmond Ct 35 E1
  Richmond Ter
Richmond St 34D1
Richmond Ter 34D1
Richmond Wk 34D1
Richmondhill Ct 34A1
Richmondhill 34A1
  Gdns
Richmondhill Pl 34A1
Richmondhill Rd 34A1
Ritchie Pl 32 C2
Riverside Dr 34D6
Riverside Ter 34 C6
Rockall Pl 35H5
Rockall Rd 35H5
Rodger's Wk 35 E1

Rose Pl 34D2
Rose St 34D2
Rose St 34D2
Rosebank Gdns 35 E3
  Rosebank Ter
Rosebank Pl 34D4
Rosebank Ter 35 E4
Rosebery St 34 B1
Rosehill Av 32A4
Rosehill Ct 32A5
Rosehill Cres 32 B4
Rosehill Dr 32A4
Rosehill Pl 32 B4
Rosehill Ter 32 B4
Rosemount Pl 34 C1
Rosemount Sq 34D1
  Richmond St
Rosemount Ter 34D1
Rosemount Viaduct 34D2
Roslin Pl 35G1
Roslin St 33G6
Roslin Ter 33 F6
Rowan Rd 32A5
Rubislaw Pl 34D3
Rubislaw Ter 34 C3
Rubislaw Ter La 34 C3
Ruby La 35 E2
  North Silver St
Ruby Pl 35 E2
  North Silver St
Russell Rd 35 F4
Ruthrie Ct 34 B6
Ruthrieston Circle 34 C6
Ruthrieston Cres 34 C6
Ruthrieston Pl 34 C6
Ruthrieston Rd 34 B6

S
St. Andrew Ct 35 E1
  St. Andrew St
St. Andrew St 35 E1
St. Catharines 34D3
  Wynd
St. Clair St 35 F1
St. Clement St 35G2
St. Clements Pl 35H2
  St. Clement St
St. Johns Pl 35 E3
  Academy St
St. Machar Ct 32 C2
  Montgomery Cres
St. Machar Dr 32D4
St. Machar Ind Est 32D3
St. Machar Pl 33 F3
St. Machar Rd 32D3
St. Mary's Ct 35 E2
  Union Wynd
St. Mary's Pl 35 E3
St. Nicholas La 35 F2
  Schoolhill
St. Nicholas 35 F2
  Shop Cen
St. Nicholas St 35 F2
  Schoolhill
St. Ninians Ct 33 F3
St. Ninians Pl 33 F2
St. Paul St 35 F1
  Gallowgate
St. Peter La 33 F6
St. Peter St 33 F6
St. Peter's Gate 33 F5
St. Peter's Pl 33 F5
St. Swithin Row 34 B3
St. Swithin St 34 B3
Salisbury Ct 34 C5
Salisbury Pl 34 C5
Salisbury Ter 34 B5
Sandilands Dr 32 C3
School Av 33 F4
School Dr 33 F4
School Pl 33 F4
  School Dr
School Rd 33 F4
School Ter 33 F4
School Wk 33 F4
Schoolhill 35 E2
Scotstown Gdns 33 F1
Seaforth Rd 33 F6
Seamount Ct 35 F1
  Gallowgate
Seamount Rd 35 F1
Seaton Av 33 F3
Seaton Cres 33G3
Seaton Dr 33 F3
Seaton Gdns 33 F3
Seaton Ho 33G3
Seaton Pl 33 F3
Seaton Pl E 33 F3
Seaton Rd 33 F4
Seaton Wk 33 F3
Seaview Ho 33G4
Seaview Rd 33 F1
Shiprow 35 F2
Shoe La 35 F1
  Queen St
Shore Brae 35 F2
  Shiprow
Shore La 35G2
Short Loanings 34D1

Sinclair Pl 35H4
Sinclair Rd 35G4
Skene La 34D2
Skene Pl 34D2
  Skene St
Skene Sq 34D1
Skene St 34D2
Skene Ter 35 E2
Smithfield La 32A3
Smithfield Rd 32 B3
Society La 32 B3
South Anderson Dr 34 B6
South College St 35 F3
South Constitution 35G1
  St
  Constitution St
South Crown St 35 E4
South Esplanade E 35G4
South Esplanade W 35 F4
South Grampian 35G5
  Circle
South Mile End 34D5
South Mt St 34D1
South Silver St 35 E2
  Union St
South Wk 32A5
  Ash-hill Dr
Spa St 35 E1
Spademill La 34A3
Spademill Rd 34A3
Spital 33 E5
Spital Wk 33 E5
Spring Gdn 35 E1
Springbank Pl 35 E3
  Springbank St
Springbank St 35 E3
Springbank Ter 35 E3
Stafford St 32D6
Stanley St 34 C3
Station Rd 32 B2
Stell Rd 35 F3
Stevenson Ct 34D2
  Stevenson St
Stevenson St 34D2
Stewart Pk Ct 32A4
Stewart Pk Pl 32A4
Stirling St 35 F2
  Guild St
Strathbeg Pl 33 E1
  Davan Pl
Strawberry Bk Par 34D3
Sugarhouse La 35G2
  Mearns St
Summer St 34D2
Summer St 32 B3
  (Woodside)
Summerfield Pl 35 F1
  Summerfield Ter
Summerfield Ter 35 F1
Sunnybank Pl 33 E5
Sunnybank Rd 33 E5
Sunnyside Av 33 E5
Sunnyside Gdns 33 E5
Sunnyside Rd 32D5
Sunnyside Ter 33 E5
Sunnyside Wk 33 E5
  Sunnybank Pl
Sycamore Pl 35 E5

T
Tanfield Av 32 C3
Tanfield Ct 32 C3
  Tanfield Wk
Tanfield Wk 32 C3
Tarbothill Rd 32D1
Tedder Rd 32D3
Tedder St 32D3
Theatre La 35G2
  Regent Quay
Thistle Ct 34D2
Thistle La 34D2
Thistle Pl 34D3
Thistle St 34D3
Thomas Glover Pl 33 E1
Thoms Ct 33 E4
  High St
Thoms Pl 33 E4
  High St
Thomson St 34 C1
Thomson St La 34 C1
  Loanhead Pl
Thorngrove Av 34A5
Thorngrove Ct 34A5
Thorngrove Cres 34A5
Thorngrove Pl 34A5
Tillydrone Av 33 E3
Tillydrone Ct 32D2
Tillydrone Rd 33 E3
Tillydrone Ter 32D3
Trinity La 35 F2
  Exchange St
Trinity Quay 35 F2
Trinity St 35 F2
  Rennies Wynd
Tullos Circle 35G5
Tullos Cres 35H5
Tullos Pl 35H5

U
Union Br 35 E2
  Union St
Union Glen 34D3

Union Glen Ct 34D3
  Union Glen
Union Gro 34 C3
Union Gro Ct 34 B4
  Union Gro
Union Row 34 C3
Union Row 34D3
Union St 34D3
Union Ter 35 E2
Union Wynd 34D2
University Rd 33 E4
Upper Denburn 34D2
Upperkirkgate 35 F2
Urquhart La 33 F6
Urquhart Pl 33G6
Urquhart Rd 33 F6
Urquhart St 33G6
Urquhart Ter 33G6

V
Victoria Br 35G3
Victoria Rd 35G4
Victoria St 34D2
View Ter 34D1
Virginia Ct 35 F2
  Justice St
Virginia St 35 F2

W
Wagrills La 33 E4
  High St
Wales St 35G2
Walker La 35G4
Walker Pl 35G4
Walker Rd 35 F5
Wallfield Cres 34 C2
Wallfield Pl 34 C2
Wapping St 35 E2
Water La 35 F2
  Mearns St
Waterloo Quay 35G2
Watson La 34 C1
Watson St 34 C1
Wavell Cres 32 C2
Waverley La 34D2
Waverley Pl 34D3
Weighhouse Sq 35G2
  Virginia St
Wellington Brae 35 F4
Wellington Br 35 F5
Wellington Pl 35 E3
Wellington Rd 35 F5
Wellington St 35H2
West Craibstone St 35 E3
  Bon Accord Ter
West Mt St 34D1
West N St 35 F1
Westburn Ct 34D1
  Westburn Rd
Westburn Cres 32 B6
Westburn Dr 32 B5
Westburn Pk 32 C6
Westburn Rd 34 C1
Western Rd 32 C3
Westfield Rd 34 C2
Westfield Ter 34 C2
Whinhill Gdns 35 E5
Whinhill Gate 35 E4
Whinhill Rd 34D5
Whitehall Ms 34 C2
  Whitehall Pl
Whitehall Pl 34 B2
Whitehall Rd 34 B2
Whitehall Ter 34 C2
Whitehouse St 34D2
Willowbank Rd 34D2
Willowdale Pl 35 F1
Willowgate Cl 34D3
  Hardgate
Windmill Brae 35 E2
Windmill La 35 E2
  Windmill Brae
Windsor Pl 34D2
  Victoria St
Wingate Pl 32D3
Wingate Rd 32D3
Woolmanhill 35 F1
Wright's & 33 E4
  Cooper's Pl
  High St

Y
York Pl 35H2
York St 35H2

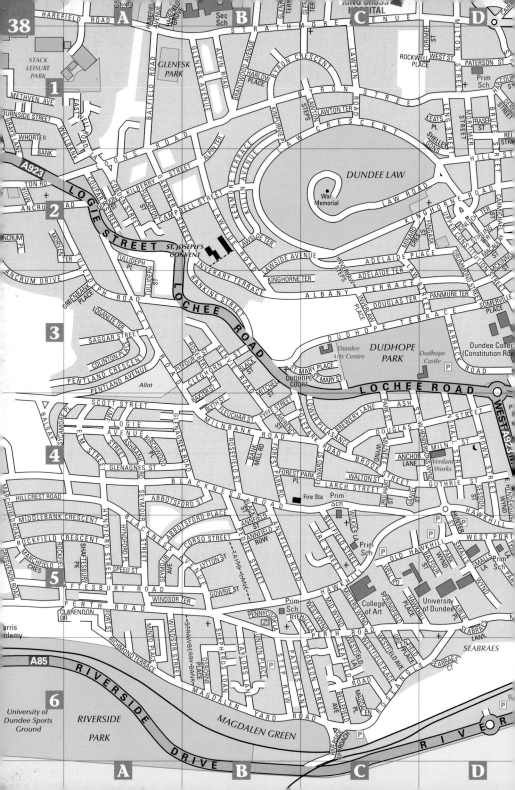

DUNDEE

E F G H

1

Maryfield House

Dundee College
(Melrose Terrace)

Morgan Academy

BAXTER

Maryfield Terrace

Madeira St

Prim Sch

Janefield PL

FORFAR ROAD

A92

Gibson Ter

Wynnewood Rd

Chalmers St

Wortley

PARK

HINDMARCH AVE

DENS PARK
(Dundee FC)

TANNADICE PARK
(Dundee United)

Strathmore Street

Melrose Terrace

Sandeman Place

Cardock St

Pitkerro Road

Baxter Park Terrace

Morgan St

2

Prim Sch

DENS ROAD

B960

Thistle
St

Kincaldrum Place

Caldrum Ter

St Salvador St

Prim Sch

Ellen's Lane

DENS ROAD

Dura St

ARTHURSTONE TER

ALBERT STREET

A929

Park Avenue

McGill St

Morgan St

Kenmore Ter

Craigie

Raglan St

ARBROATH ROAD

B959

Springhill

Baffin Ter

Eden Ter

Eden St

3

Wellington Street

William Street

Laing St

Cotton Road

W. Lyon St

Lyon Street

Victoria St

Mary Slessor Sq

Crescent Street

Crescent St

KING ST

PRINCES STREET

Constable Street

Blackscroft

Foundry Lane

Peep-O-Day Lane

Robertson St

Lilyb.

St. Matthew Lane

Watson St

S. Baffin Street

BROUGHTY FERRY ROAD

Melville Lane

EAST DOCK STREET

A92

4

University of Abertay Dundee

Wellgate Centre

Cowgate

McManus Galleries

EAST MARKETGAIT

Camperdown Street

CAMPERDOWN DOCK

VICTORIA DOCK

Frigate Unicorn

W. Wharf Rd

S. Victoria Dock Rd

Timber

5

THE HOWFF GRAVEYARD

Forum Shopping Centre

CITY SQUARE

SOUTH MARKETGAIT

Castle St

Dock St

Kingsway

Victoria Dock Rd

Toll (South only)

FIRTH OF TAY

DUNDEE

Overgate Centre

Olympia Leisure Centre

Earl Grey Place

R.R.S. Discovery

Discovery Point

Discovery Quay

DISCOVERY DRIVE

TAY ROAD BRIDGE

A92

6

E F G H

DUNDEE

INDEX TO STREETS

A

Abbotsford Pl 38 A5
Abbotsford St 38 A4
Adelaide Pl 38 C2
Adelaide Ter 38 C3
Airlie Pl 38 D5
Albany Ter 38 C3
Albert Sq 39 F4
  Panmure St
Albert St 39 H2
Alexander St 39 E2
Alpin Rd 38 B1
Alpin Ter 38 B2
Alva Sq 39 E2
Anchor La 38 C4
Ann St 39 E3
Annfield Rd 38 B5
Annfield Row 38 B5
Annfield St 38 B5
Arbroath Rd 39 H2
Arklay St 39 F1
Arthur St 39 E3
Arthurstone Ter 39 G2
Artillery La 38 D5
Ash La 38 C4
  Ash St
Ash St 38 C4
Ashbank Rd 38 A4

B

Baffin St 39 H2
Baffin Ter 39 H2
  Baffin St
Baldovan Ter 39 H1
Balfield Rd 38 A1
Balfour St 38 D5
Balgayview 38 A2
  Gdns
Balmore St 39 G2
Baltic Gdns 38 B6
  Patons La
Baltic La 39 E3
Bank Mill Rd 38 B4
Bank St 39 E4
Barrack Rd 38 D3
Barrack St 39 E4
Baxter Pk Ter 39 H1
Baxter St 38 B4
Bell St 39 E4
Bellefield Av 38 C6
Bellfield St 38 C5
Benvie Rd 38 B3
Birchwood Pl 38 A4
Black St 38 B3
Blackness Av 38 A5
Blackness Rd 38 A4
Blackness St 38 A5
Blackness Ter 38 A5
Blackscroft 39 G3
Blaikies Ms 39 E2
  Alexander St
Blinshall St 38 D4
Blyth Pl 38 B4
Blyth St 38 B4
Bonnet Hill Pl 39 F3
  Eadies Rd
Bonnethill Ct 39 E3
  Hilltown Ter
Bonnybank Rd 39 F3
Brantwood Av 38 B1

Brantwood Pl 38 B1
  Brantwood Av
Brewery La 38 C4
Brook St 38 C4
Brougham 39 G2
  Gdns
Broughty 39 H3
  Ferry Rd
Brown 39 G2
  Constable St
Brown St 38 D4
Bruce St 38 D1
Buchanan St 39 G2
Bucklemaker Ct 38 D1
  Harcourt St
Burgess St 38 D1
Butterburn Ct 38 D1
  Strathmartine Rd
Butterburn Sq 38 D1
Byron Cres 38 B1
Byron St 38 B1

C

Caldrum St 39 E2
Caldrum Ter 39 E2
Callender Gdns 39 G3
Campbell St 38 A2
Camperdown 39 G4
  St
Candle La 39 F4
Canning Pl 38 D1
Canning St 38 D1
Cardean St 39 G2
Carmichael Ct 38 D2
Carmichael 38 D2
  Gdns
Carmichael St 38 D2
  Ann St
Carnegie Sq 39 E2
Carnegie Twr 39 F2
  Alexander St
Castle St 39 F4
Catherine St 39 G1
Chapel St 39 E4
  Meadowside
Church St 39 E2
City Rd 38 A3
City Sq 39 F4
Clarendon Dr 38 A5
Clarendon Ter 38 A5
Cleghorn St 38 B3
Clepington St 39 F1
Cobden Pl 38 A2
Cobden St 38 A2
Colinton Pl 38 A3
Commercial St 39 F4
Constable St 39 G3
Constitution Rd 38 D3
Constitution St 38 D3
Constitution 38 D3
  Ter
Corso St 38 B5
Cotton Rd 39 F2
Coupar St 38 A2
Court St 39 G1
Courthouse Sq 38 D3
Coutties Wynd 39 E5
Cowan St 39 G2
Cowgate 39 F4

Craigie St 39 H2
Crescent La 39 G3
Crescent St 39 G3
Crichton St 39 F5
Cross La 38 D5
Cross Row 38 D5
Cunningham St 39 G2

D

Dalfield Ct 39 E3
  Hilltown Ter
Daniel St 38 C4
Dens Brae 39 G3
Dens Rd 39 E1
Dens St 39 G3
Derby St 38 D1
Discovery 39 E6
  Quay
Dock St 39 F4
Dons Rd 39 E3
Douglas St 38 C4
Douglas Ter 38 C3
Drummond St 38 D2
Dudhope Ct 38 B3
Dudhope 39 E3
  Cres Rd
Dudhope St 39 E3
Dudhope Ter 38 C3
Dundonald St 39 F1
Dura St 39 G2
Dykehead Pl 39 G2

E

Eadies Rd 39 F3
Earl Grey Pl 39 F5
Eassons Angle 38 B4
East Dock St 39 G4
East 38 D4
  Hendersons Wynd
East Marketgait 39 F3
East Somerville 38 D3
  Pl
East Whale La 39 G3
Eastwell Rd 38 A1
Edward St 38 C4
Eliza St 39 G1
Ellen St 39 F2
Elm St 38 A4
Erskine St 39 G2
Euclid Cres 39 E4
Euclid St 39 E4
Exchange St 39 F4

F

Fairbairn St 39 F1
Ferguson St 39 G3
Fingask St 38 D2
Fleuchar St 38 B4
Fords La 38 B5
  Perth Rd
Forebank Rd 39 F3
Forebank St 39 F3
  Forebank Rd
Forebank Ter 39 F3
  Forebank Rd
Forest Pk Pl 38 B4
Forest Pk Rd 38 B4
Forester St 39 E4

Forfar Rd 39 H1
Fort St 38 A5
Foundry La 39 G3
Fraser St 38 D1
Fullarton St 38 A2
Fyffe St 38 B4

G

Gardner St 38 A2
Gardners La 38 C3
Garland Pl 38 D3
Gellatly St 39 F4
Glamis St 39 E2
Glenagnes Rd 38 A4
Glenagnes St 38 A4
Glenesk Av 38 B1
Glenisla Ter 38 B1
Gordon Sq 38 A2
Gordon St 38 A2
Gowrie St 38 B5
Graham Pl 39 G3
Greenbank Pl 38 A3
Greenfield Pl 38 C5
Greenmarket 39 E5
Guthrie St 38 D4

H

Harcourt St 38 D1
Harlow Pl 38 B1
Harriet St 39 G1
Hastings Pl 38 D1
Hawkhill 38 C5
Hawkhill Pl 38 C5
High Mill Ct 38 B6
High St 39 E5
Hill Sq 39 E2
Hill St 38 D2
Hillbank Gdns 39 F2
Hillbank Pl 39 F2
  Hillbank Rd
Hillbank Rd 39 F2
Hilltown 39 E2
Hilltown Ct 39 E3
  Hilltown Ter
Hilltown Ter 39 E3
Horse Wynd 39 F4
Horsewater 38 D4
  Wynd
Hunter St 39 E2
Hyndford Pl 38 A4
Hyndford St 38 A4

I

Inverary Ter 38 B2
Inverlaw Pl 38 C3
Inverlaw Steps 38 C2
Isla St 39 E1

J

Jamaica Sq 39 F2
  Ann St
Jamaica St 39 F2
Jamaica Twr 39 F2
  Alexander St
James St 39 E2
Janefield Pl 39 H1
Johnston St 38 D4

K

Keats Pl 38 D1
Kemback St 39 H2
Kenmore Ter 38 B2
Kennet Wk 39 E2
Kilberry St 38 A2
Killin Av 38 B2
Kincaldrum Pl 39 E2
Kincardine St 38 C5
King St 39 F3
King William St 39 F4
Kinghorne Ct 38 D2
  Kinghorne Rd
Kinghorne Pl 38 D2
  Kinghorne Rd
Kinghorne Rd 38 C2
Kinghorne Ter 38 B3
Kinghorne Wk 38 D2
Kinloch St 38 D2
Kinloch Ter 38 D2
  Stirling Av
Kinnaird St 38 D2
Kinpurnie Pl 38 B1
Kirk La 39 F3

L

Laburn St 39 E3
  Dudhope Cres Rd
Ladywell Av 39 F3
Laing Pl 39 F2
  Laing St
Laing St 39 F2
Lambs La 39 E2
Langlands St 39 G2
Larch St 38 C4
Laurel Bk 39 E3
Law Cres 38 B1
Law Rd 38 C2
Law St 38 C2
Lawrence St 38 B4
Lawside Av 38 B3
Lawside Rd 38 B2
Lawside Ter 38 B2
Lawson Pl 38 D2
Lawton Rd 38 C1
Lawton Steps 38 C1
Lawton Ter 38 C1
Leng St 38 D1
Lilybank Rd 39 H3
Lilybank Ter 39 H3
Lime St 38 A4
Lochee Rd 38 C3
Loganlee Ter 38 A3
Logie Av 38 A4
Logie Gdns 38 A4
Logie St 38 A2
Loons Rd 38 A2
Lorimer St 38 D1
Lower 38 C4
  Pleasance
Lynnewood Pl 39 H1
Lyon St 39 G2
Lytton St 38 B5

M

Macaulay St 38 D2
Magdalen Pl 38 C6
Magdalen 38 B6
  Yd Rd

Name	Grid
Main St	39 E2
Mains Rd	39 E1
Maitland St	39 G2
Malcolm St	39 G2
Malcolms Penn	38 D4
Marine Par	39 G3
Martingale	39 G3
Gdns	
Victoria Rd	
Mary Slessor	39 G3
Sq	
Maryann La	39 F4
Maryfield Ter	39 H1
Maxwelltown	39 E2
Twr	
Alexander St	
McDonald St	39 E3
McGill St	39 H2
McGonagall Sq	38 B6
Patons La	
McKinnon St	38 D2
McVicars La	38 C5
Meadow Entry	39 F4
Commercial St	
Meadow La	39 F4
Meadow Pl	39 E3
Bldgs	
Victoria Rd	
Meadowside	39 E4
Melrose Ter	39 G1
Melville La	39 H3
Mid Rd	39 E1
Mid Wynd	38 C5
Middle St	39 G3
Millers Wynd	38 C5
Miln St	38 D4
Milnbank Rd	38 B4
Milnes E Wynd	38 C4
Milton St	38 D1
Minard Cres	38 C2
Minto Pl	38 A5
Mitchell St	38 B3
Molison St	39 G1
Morgan Pl	39 H2
Morgan St	39 H1
Mortimer St	38 D1
Murraygate	39 F4

N

Name	Grid
Neish St	39 F1
Nelson St	39 F2
Nelson Ter	39 F3
Nelson St	
Nethergate	38 D5
New Inn Entry	39 E4
High St	
Nicoll St	39 E4
North Ellen St	39 F2
North	39 G2
Erskine St	
North	39 E2
George St	
North Isla St	39 F1
North	39 E4
Lindsay St	
North	38 D4
Marketgait	
North	38 D2
Somerville Pl	
North St	39 E1
North	39 F2
Wellington St	
North	39 F2
William St	

O

Name	Grid
Ogilvie St	39 G2
Ogilvie's Rd	39 E2
Old Hawkhill	38 C5
Old Kings	38 A2
Cross Rd	
Osborne Pl	38 B6
Overgate La	39 E5

P

Name	Grid
Palais Ct	39 E5
Panmure St	39 E4
Panmure Ter	38 D3
Paradise Rd	39 E3
Park Av	39 H2
Park Pl	38 D5
Park St	38 C4
Park Wynd	38 D5
Parker St	38 D3
Paterson St	38 D1
Patons La	38 B6
Patrick Pl	38 B6
Peddie St	38 A5
Peep O'day La	39 G3
Pennycook La	38 B5
Pentland Av	38 A3
Pentland Cres	38 A3
Perth Rd	38 C5
Peter St	39 F4
Pitfour St	38 A3
Pitkerro Rd	39 H1
Pleasance Ct	38 C4
Douglas St	
Pole St	38 B4
Polepark Rd	38 B4
Powrie Pl	39 E3
Princes St	39 G3
Prospect Pl	39 E3

Q

Name	Grid
Queen St	39 F3

R

Name	Grid
Raglan St	39 H2
Rankine St	38 B3
Rattray St	39 E4
Reform St	39 E4
Reid Sq	38 D1
Reid St	
Reid St	38 D2
Richmond Ter	38 A6
Ritchie's La	38 B5
Perth Rd	
Riverside Dr	38 D6
Robertson St	39 H3
Rockwell Pl	38 C1
Roseangle	38 C6
Rosebank Pl	39 E3
Rosebank Rd	39 E3
Rosebank St	39 E2
Rosebery St	38 B3
Rosefield St	38 B4
Rosemount Ter	38 D3
Upper	
Constitution St	
Royal Ex Ct	39 F4
Panmure St	
Royal Ex La	39 E4
Meadowside	
Russell Pl	38 D1
Ryehill La	38 B5

S

Name	Grid
Saggar St	38 A3
St. Andrews La	39 F4
St. Andrews St	
St. Andrews St	39 F4
St. Davids La	38 D4
West Marketgait	
St. Mary Pl	38 B3
St. Mary St	38 C3
St. Matthews	39 H3
La	
St. Peter St	38 B5
St. Roques La	39 G3
St. Salvador St	39 E2
Salem St	39 E3
Constitution Rd	
Scott St	38 A4
Seabraes	38 D6
Seabraes Ct	38 D6
Seabraes La	38 D5
Seafield Cl	38 C6
Seafield La	38 C6
Seafield Rd	38 C6
Seagate	39 F4
Session St	38 D4
Seymour Av	38 A5
Seymour St	38 A4
Shaftesbury Pk	38 A5
Shaftesbury Pl	38 A5
Shaftesbury	38 A5
Ter	
Shelley Gdns	38 D1
Shepherds	38 B5
Loan	
Shore Ter	39 F4
Castle St	
Sibbald St	39 F1
Smalls La	38 D5
Smalls Wynd	38 D5
Soap Wks La	39 E3
Somerville Pl	38 D3
South Baffin St	39 H3
South	39 F3
George St	
South	39 F5
Marketgait	
South Tay St	38 D5
South Victoria	39 G4
Dock Rd	
South Ward Rd	39 E4
Speed St	38 A5
Spinners Wynd	38 B6
Taylors La	
Springfield	38 C5
Step Row	38 B6
Stephen's Yd	38 B6
Stirling Av	38 D2
Stirling St	38 D2
Stirling Ter	38 D2
Stirling Av	
Stobswell Rd	39 G1
Strathmartine	38 D1
Rd	
Strathmore Av	38 B1
Strathmore St	39 F1
Strawberry Bk	38 B5
Sugarhouse	39 F3
Wynd	

T

Name	Grid
Taits La	38 B5
Tannadice Ct	39 F1
Tannadice St	
Tannadice St	39 E1
Tay Rd Br	39 G5
Tay Sq	39 E5
Tay St La	39 E5
Nethergate	
Tayfield Pl	38 B6
Patons La	
Taylors La	38 B6
Temple La	38 D5
Thistle St	39 E1
Thomson St	38 C6
Timber St	39 G4
Trades La	39 F4
Tullideph Pl	38 A2
Tullideph Rd	38 A2
Tullideph St	38 A3
Tulloch Ct	39 E3
Hilltown Ter	

U

Name	Grid
Union Pl	38 B5
Union St	39 E5
Union Ter	38 D3
Upper	38 D2
Constitution St	
Ure St	38 C5
Urquhart St	38 C4

V

Name	Grid
Victoria Rd	39 E3
Victoria St	39 G3

W

Name	Grid
Walker's Mill	39 F1
Wallace St	39 G3
Walton St	38 C4
Ward Rd	38 D4
Watson St	39 H3
Watsons La	38 C4
Hawkhill	
Weavers Yd	39 G3
Well Rd	38 C5
Wellbank La	38 A1
Wellgate Cen	39 F3
Wellington Sq	39 F3
Ann St	
Wellington St	39 F2
Wellington	39 F2
Twr	
Alexander St	
West Bell St	38 D4
West	38 D4
Hendersons Wynd	
West Lyon St	39 G2
West	38 D4
Marketgait	
West Port	38 D5
West	38 D3
Somerville Pl	
West St	38 D1
West Victoria	39 G4
Dock Rd	
West Wf Rd	39 G4
West Wynd	38 C5
Westfield Av	38 C5
Westfield La	38 C6
Westfield Pl	38 C6
Wetherby Pl	38 C1
Whistler's Way	39 E3
Powrie Pl	
Whitehall Cres	39 E5
Whitehall St	39 E5
Wilkies La	38 C4
William	39 E3
Barclay Sq	
William St	39 F2
Willison St	39 E4
Windsor Pl	38 B6
Magdalen Yd Rd	
Windsor St	38 A5
Windsor Ter	38 A5
Wishart St	38 D2
Stirling Av	
Wolseley St	39 G1

Y

Name	Grid
Yeaman Shore	39 E5
Union St	

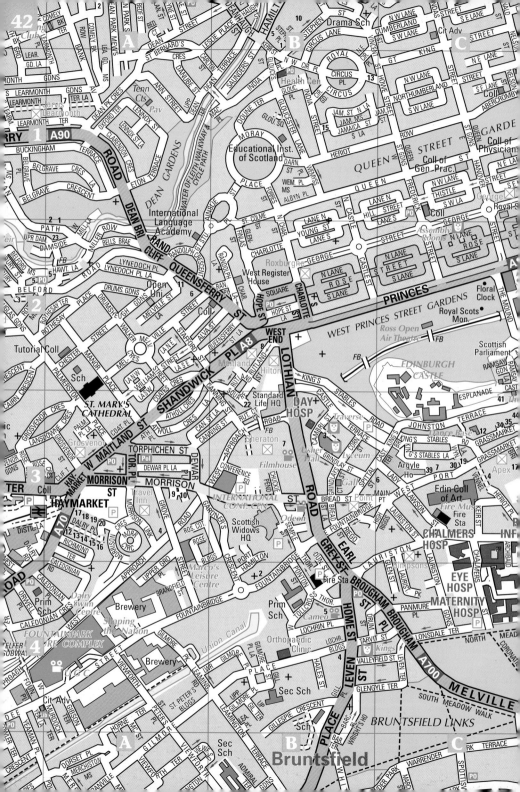

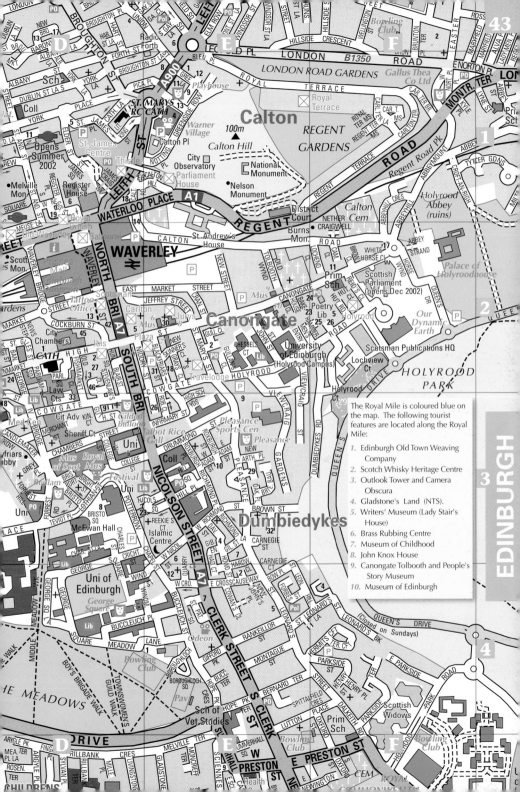

The Royal Mile is coloured blue on the map. The following tourist features are located along the Royal Mile:

1. Edinburgh Old Town Weaving Company
2. Scotch Whisky Heritage Centre
3. Outlook Tower and Camera Obscura
4. Gladstone's Land (NTS).
5. Writers' Museum (Lady Stair's House)
6. Brass Rubbing Centre
7. Museum of Childhood
8. John Knox House
9. Canongate Tolbooth and People's Story Museum
10. Museum of Edinburgh

EDINBURGH

43

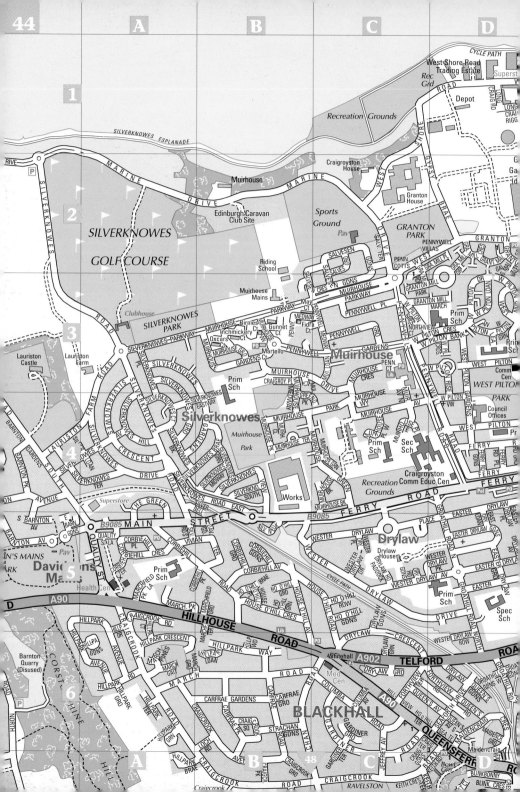

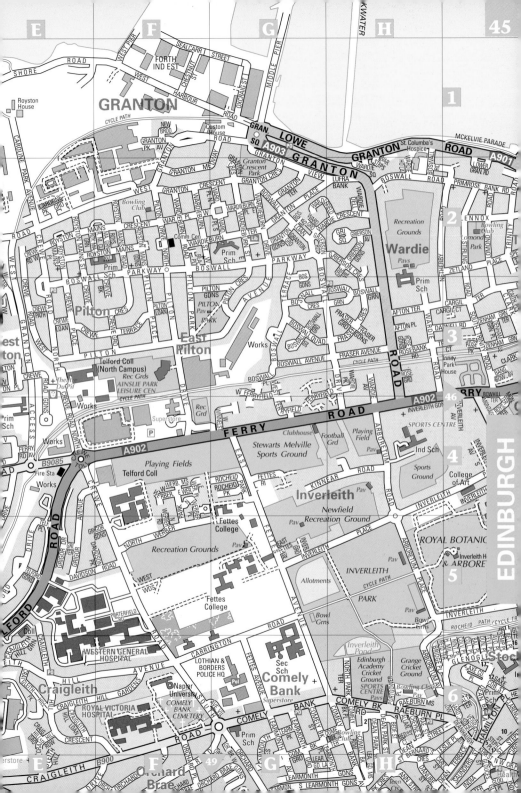

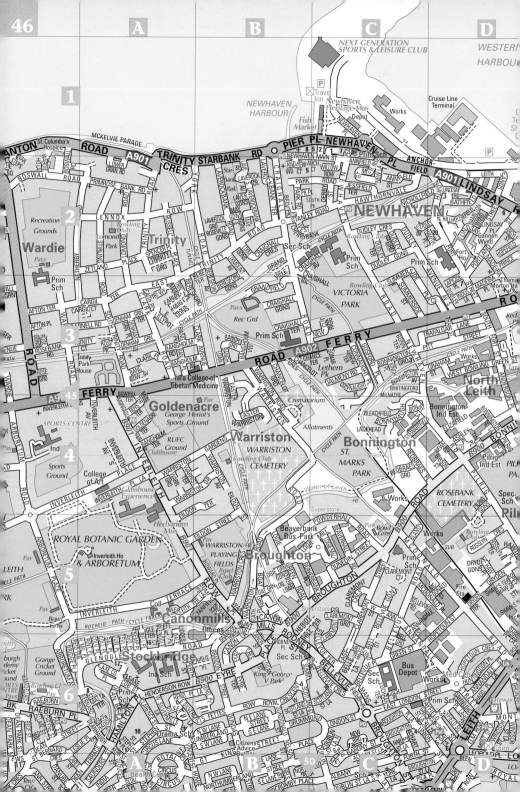

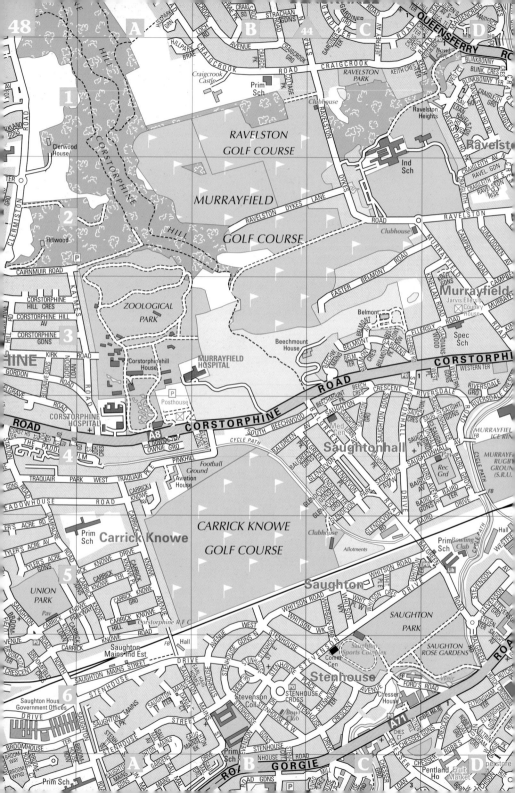

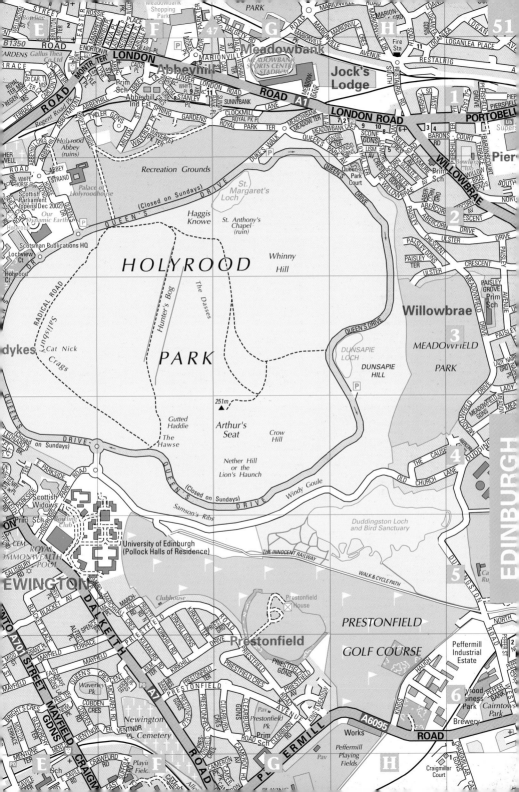

INDEX TO STREETS

52

Note: There are street names in this index which are followed by a number in **bold**. These numbers can be found on the map where there is insufficient space to show the street name in full.

A

Abbey La	51 F1
Abbey Strand	43 F2
Abbey St	51 F1
Abbeyhill	43 F2
Abbeyhill Cres	43 F2
Abbeyhill Ind Est	51 F1
Abbeymount	43 F1
Abbotsford Ct	49 H6
Abbotsford Cres	49 H6
Abbotsford Pk	49 H6
Abercorn Cres	51 H2
Abercorn Dr	51 H2
Abercorn Gro	51 H2
Abercorn Rd	51 H2
Abercromby Pl	42 C1
Abinger Gdns	49 E3
Academy Pk	47 F4
Academy St	47 F4
Admiral Ter	50 A5
Admiralty St	47 E2
Advocates Cl **1**	43 D2
Afton Pl	45 H3
Afton Ter	45 H3
Agnew Ter	46 C3
Ainslie Pl	42 A1
Aird's Cl	42 C3
Airlie Pl	46 B6
Aitkenhill	48 C6
Albany La	43 D1
Albany St	43 D1
Albany St La	43 D1
Albert Dock	47 F2
Albert Pl	46 D6
Albert Rd	47 G3
Albert St	47 E5
Albert Ter	49 H6
Albion	47 F6
Business Cen	
Albion Pl	47 F6
Albion Rd	47 F6
Albion Ter	47 F6
Albyn Pl	42 B1
Alderbank Gdns	49 F6
Alderbank Pl	49 F6
Alderbank Ter	49 F6
Alemoor Cres	47 G5
Alemoor Pk	47 G5
Alexander Dr	49 E5
Alfred Pl	51 E5
Allan St	45 H6
Allanfield	47 E6
Almondbank Ter	49 F6
Alva Pl	51 F1
Alva St	42 A2
Alvanley Ter **1**	50 A5
Anchor Cl **45**	43 D2
Anchorfield	46 C2
Anderson Pl	46 D3
Andrew Wd Ct	46 B2
Angle Pk Ter	49 G5
Ann St	42 A1
Annandale St	46 C5
Annandale St La	46 D6
Annfield	46 C2
Annfield St	46 C2
Antigua St **6**	46 D6
Appin Ter	49 E6
Arboretum Av	45 H6
Arboretum Pl	45 H5
Arboretum Rd	45 H4
Archibald Pl	42 C3
Arden St	50 B5
Ardmillan Pl	49 G5
Ardmillan Ter	49 F5
Ardmillan Ter La **1**	49 G5
Argyle Pk Ter	50 C5
Argyle Pl	50 C5
Argyle St	46 D2
Argyll Ter **14**	42 A3
Arthur St	47 E5
Arthur St La	47 E5
Ashley Gro	49 F6
Ashley Pl	46 D4
Ashley Ter	49 F6

Ashville Ter	47 G5
Assembly St	47 F3
Atholl Cres	42 A3
Atholl Cres La	42 A3
Atholl Pl	42 A3
Atholl Ter **15**	42 A3
Auchinleck Ct	46 C2
Auchinleck's	46 B2
Brae **5**	
Avenue Vil	45 G6
Avondale Pl	46 A6

B

Back Dean	49 G2
Baird Av	48 D4
Baird Dr	48 D5
Baird Gdns	48 D4
Baird Gro	48 D4
Baird Ter	48 D4
Bakehouse Cl	43 E2
Baker's Pl **1**	46 A6
Balbirnie Pl	49 F3
Balfour Pl	46 D4
Balfour St	47 E4
Balgreen Av	48 B4
Balgreen Gdns	48 B4
Balgreen Pk	48 B4
Balgreen Rd	48 D5
Ballantyne La **1**	47 E3
Ballantyne Rd	47 E3
Balmoral Pl	46 A6
Baltic St	47 F3
Bangholm Av	46 A3
Bangholm	46 A3
Bower Av	
Bangholm Gro	46 B3
Bangholm Loan	46 B3
Bangholm Pk	46 A3
Bangholm Pl	46 A3
Bangholm Rd	46 A3
Bangholm Ter	46 A4
Bangholm Vw	46 B3
Bangor Rd	46 D3
Bank St	43 D2
Barclay Pl	42 B4
Barclay Ter	50 A5
Baronscourt Rd	51 H1
Barony Pl **17**	46 C6
Barony St	46 C6
Bath Rd	47 G3
Bathfield	46 D2
Baxter's Pl **1**	43 E1
Beaufort Rd	50 C4
Beaverbank	46 B5
Business Pk	
Beaverbank Pl	46 C5
Beaverhall Rd	46 C5
Bedford Ct	45 H6
Bedford St	45 H6
Beechmount Cres	48 C4
Beechmount Pk	48 C4
Beechwood Mains	48 C3
Beechwood Ter	47 G5
Belford Av	49 F1
Belford Br	49 G2
Belford Gdns	49 F1
Belford Ms	49 G2
Belford Pk	49 G2
Belford Pl	49 F2
Belford Rd	49 G2
Belford Ter **1**	49 G2
Belgrave Cres	49 G1
Belgrave Cres La	49 G1
Belgrave Ms	49 G1
Belgrave Pl	49 G1
Bell Pl	46 A6
Bellevue	46 C6
Bellevue Cres	46 C6
Bellevue Gdns	46 C5
Bellevue Gro	46 C6
Bellevue La	46 C6
Bellevue Pl	46 C6
Bellevue Rd	46 C6
Bellevue St	46 C6
Bellevue Ter	46 C5

Bells Brae	42 A2
Bell's Mills	49 G2
Bell's Wynd **2**	43 D2
Belmont Av	48 C3
Belmont Cres	48 C3
Belmont Gdns	48 C3
Belmont Pk	48 C3
Belmont Ter	48 C3
Belmont Vw	48 C3
Belvedere Pk	46 B2
Beresford Av	46 B2
Beresford Gdns	46 B3
Beresford Pl	46 A3
Beresford Ter	46 A3
Bernard St	47 F2
Bernard Ter	43 E4
Birnies Ct	44 B3
Blackadder Pl	45 F2
Blacket Av	51 E5
Blacket Pl	51 E5
Blackford Rd	50 B6
Blackfriars St	43 E2
Blackie Rd	47 G4
Blackwood Cres	50 D5
Blair St	43 D2
Blandfield	46 C5
Blantyre Ter	49 H6
Bleachfield	46 C4
Blenheim Pl	43 E1
Blinkbonny Av	49 E1
Blinkbonny Cres	49 E1
Blinkbonny Gdns	49 E1
Blinkbonny Gro	49 E1
Blinkbonny Gro W	49 E1
Blinkbonny Rd	49 E1
Blinkbonny Ter	48 D1
Boat Grn	46 B5
Bonar Pl	46 C3
Bonnington Av	46 C3
Bonnington Gait **1**	46 D4
Bonnington Gro	46 C3
Bonnington	46 D4
Ind Est	
Bonnington Rd	46 D4
Bonnington Rd La	46 D4
Bonnington Ter	46 C3
Bonnyhaugh	46 C4
Bonnyhaugh La	46 C4
Boothacre Cotts **2**	47 H4
Boothacre La	47 H4
Boroughloch	43 E4
Boroughloch Sq	43 E4
Borthwick Pl	49 F3
Borthwick's Cl **3**	43 D2
Boswall Av	45 G3
Boswall Cres	45 G3
Boswall Dr	45 G2
Boswall Gdns	45 G3
Boswall Grn	45 H3
Boswall Gro	45 G3
Boswall Loan	45 G2
Boswall Ms	45 G2
Boswall Parkway	45 F2
Boswall Pl	45 G3
Boswall Quad	45 G3
Boswall Rd	45 H2
Boswall Sq	45 G3
Boswall Ter	45 G3
Bothwell St	47 E6
Bowhill Ter	46 A4
Bowie's Cl **8**	47 F3
Bowling Grn, The	47 E3
Bowling La **22**	47 E3
Bowmont Pl	43 E4
Boyd's Entry **2**	43 E2
Boy's Brigade Wk	43 D4
Brandfield St	42 A4
Brandon St	46 B6
Brandon Ter	46 B6
Bread St	42 B3
Bread St La	42 B3
Breadalbane St	46 D3
Breadalbane	42 A3
Ter **16**	
Brewery La **2**	47 E3
Briarbank Ter	49 F6

Bridge Pl	45 H6
Briery Bauks	43 E3
Bright Ter **19**	42 A3
Brighton St	43 D3
Bright's Cres	51 E6
Bristo Pl	43 D3
Bristo Port	43 D3
Bristo Sq	43 D3
Broad Wynd **7**	47 F3
Broomhouse Row	48 A6
Brougham Pl	42 C4
Brougham St	42 B4
Broughton Mkt	46 C6
Broughton Pl	46 C6
Broughton Pl La	46 C6
Broughton Rd	46 C5
Broughton St	46 C6
Broughton St La	43 D1
Brown St	43 E3
Brown St La **32**	43 E3
Brown's Cl	43 F2
Brown's Pl **4**	42 C3
Brunswick Pl	46 D6
Brunswick Rd	46 D6
Brunswick St	46 D6
Brunswick St La	46 D6
Brunswick Ter **10**	47 E6
Brunton Gdns **2**	47 E6
Brunton Pl	47 E6
Brunton Ter	47 E6
Bruntsfield Av	50 A5
Bruntsfield Cres	50 A5
Bruntsfield Gdns	50 A6
Bruntsfield Pl	49 H6
Bruntsfield Ter	50 A5
Bryson Rd	49 G5
Buccleuch Pl	43 D4
Buccleuch St	43 E4
Buccleuch Ter	43 E4
Buchanan St	47 E5
Buckingham Ter	49 G1
Bull's Cl **5**	43 F2
Burgess St	47 F3
Burgess Ter	51 F6
Burlington St	47 E3
Burns St	47 F4

C

Cables Wynd	47 E3
Cables Wynd Ho	47 E3
Cadiz St	47 F3
Cadzow Pl	51 F1
Caithness Pl	46 A3
Caledonian Cres	49 G4
Caledonian Pl	42 A4
Caledonian Rd	42 A3
Calton Hill	43 E1
Calton Rd	43 E2
Cambridge Av	46 D5
Cambridge Gdns	46 D5
Cambridge St	42 B3
Cambridge	42 B3
St La **3**	
Cambusnethan St	51 G1
Cameron Ho Av	51 G6
Campbell Av	48 D3
Campbell Rd	48 D2
Campbell's Cl	43 F2
Candlemaker Row	43 D3
Canning St	42 B2
Canning St La	42 A3
Cannon Wynd	46 D2
Canon Ct **3**	46 B5
Canon La	46 B6
Canon St	46 B6
Canongate	43 E2
Canonmills	46 B5
Canonmills Br **5**	46 B5
Carberry Pl	49 F3
Carfrae Gdns	44 B6
Carfrae Gro	44 B6
Carfrae Pk	44 B6
Carfrae Rd	44 B6
Cargil Ct	45 H3
Cargil Ter	46 A3

Carlton St	42 A1
Carlton Ter	43 F1
Carlton Ter Brae	43 F1
Carlton Ter La	43 F1
Carlton Ter Ms	43 F1
Carlyle Pl	51 F1
Carnegie Ct	43 E3
Carnegie St	43 E3
Caroline Pk Av	45 E1
Caroline Pk Gro	45 E2
Carpet La	47 F3
Carrick Knowe Av	48 A4
Carrick Knowe	48 A5
Gdns	
Carrick Knowe Gro	48 A5
Carrick Knowe Hill	48 A5
Carrick Knowe Pl	48 A5
Carrick Knowe Ter	48 A5
Carrington Rd	45 F6
Carron Pl	47 G3
Carrubber's Cl **5**	43 E2
Casselbank St	47 E4
Cassel's La	47 E4
Castle St	42 B2
Castle Ter	42 C3
Castle Wynd N **41**	42 C3
Castle Wynd S **34**	42 C3
Castlehill	42 C2
Cathcart Pl	49 G4
Cathedral La	43 D1
Catherine Pl	46 B5
Causeway, The	51 H4
Causewayside	50 D5
Chalmers Bldgs **2**	42 B4
Chalmers Cl **30**	43 E2
Chalmers Cres	50 C5
Chalmers St	42 C3
Chamberlain Rd	50 A6
Chambers St	43 D3
Chancelot Cres	46 B3
Chancelot Gro	46 B3
Chancelot Ter	46 C3
Chapel La **2**	47 F3
Chapel St	43 D3
Chapel Wynd **7**	42 C3
Charles St	43 D3
Charles St La	43 D3
Charlesfield **8**	43 D3
Charlotte La	42 B2
Charlotte Sq	42 B2
Chessels Ct	43 E2
Chesser Av	48 C6
Chesser Cotts **1**	48 D6
Chesser Ct	48 C6
Chesser Gdns	48 C6
Chester St	42 A2
Chestnut St	45 F1
Cheyne St	45 H6
Chuckie Pend	42 B3
Church Hill	50 A6
Church Hill Dr	50 A6
Church Hill Pl	50 A6
Circus Gdns	42 B1
Circus La	46 A6
Circus Pl	42 B1
Citadel Pl	47 E2
Citadel St **21**	47 E2
Clarebank Cres	47 G4
Claremont Bk	46 C6
Claremont Ct	46 C5
Claremont Cres	46 C5
Claremont Gdns	47 G4
Claremont Gro	46 C5
Claremont Pk	47 G4
Claremont Rd	47 G4
Clarence St	46 A6
Clarendon Cres	42 A1
Clark Av	46 B3
Clark Pl	46 A3
Clark Rd	46 A3
Clearburn Cres	51 G6
Clearburn Gdns	51 G6
Clearburn Rd	51 G6
Clerk St	43 E4
Clifton Ter	42 A3

Name	Page	Grid
Clinton Rd	50	A6
Clockmill La	51	G1
Coalhill	47	E3
Coates Cres	42	A3
Coates Gdns	49	G3
Coates Pl	42	A3
Coatfield La	47	F3
Cobden Cres	51	E6
Cobden Rd	51	E6
Cobden Ter 18	42	A3
Coburg St	47	E3
Cochran Pl	46	C6
Cochran Ter	46	C6
Cochrane Pl 1	47	F4
Cockburn St	43	D2
Coffin La	49	G4
Coinyie Ho Cl 18	43	E2
College Wynd 9	43	D3
Collins Pl	46	A6
Coltbridge Av	49	E3
Coltbridge Gdns	49	F3
Coltbridge Millside	49	F3
Coltbridge Ter	49	E3
Coltbridge Vale	49	F3
Columba Av	44	C6
Columba Rd	44	C6
Colville Pl	46	A6
Comely Bk	45	G6
Comely Bk Av	45	H6
Comely Bk Gro	49	G1
Comely Bk Pl	45	H6
Comely Bk Pl Ms 2	45	H6
Comely Bk Rd	45	H6
Comely Bk Row	45	H6
Comely Bk St	45	G6
Comely Bk Ter	45	G6
Comely Grn Cres	51	F1
Comely Grn Pl	51	F1
Commercial St	47	E2
Commercial Wf 1	47	F2
Conference Sq	42	B3
Connaught Pl	46	C6
Considine Gdns	51	H1
Considine Ter	51	H1
Constitution Pl	47	F4
Constitution St	47	F4
Convening Ct 1	42	A2
Cooper's Cl 23	43	F2
Corbiehill Av	44	B5
Corbiehill Cres	44	A5
Corbiehill Gdns	44	B5
Corbiehill Gro	44	A5
Corbiehill Pk	44	A5
Corbiehill Pl	44	A5
Corbiehill Rd	44	A5
Corbiehill Ter	44	A5
Cornhill Ter	47	G4
Cornwall St	42	B3
Cornwallis Pl	46	B6
Coronation Wk	42	C4
Corstorphine Rd	48	B4
Corunna Pl	47	E3
Cottage Pk	48	B1
Couper St	47	E2
Cowan Rd	49	F6
Cowan's Cl	43	E4
Cowgate	43	D3
Cowgatehead	43	D3
Coxfield	48	D6
Craigcrook Av	42	C4
Craigcrook Gdns	48	C1
Craigcrook Gro	48	B1
Craigcrook Pk	48	B1
Craigcrook Pl 3	44	D6
Craigcrook Rd	48	C1
Craigcrook Sq	44	B6
Craigcrook Ter	44	C6
Craighall Av	46	B2
Craighall Bk	46	B2
Craighall Cres	46	B2
Craighall Gdns	46	B3
Craighall Rd	46	B2
Craighall Ter	46	B3
Craigleith Av N	48	D2
Craigleith Av S	48	D2
Craigleith Bk	48	D1
Craigleith Cres	48	D1
Craigleith Dr	48	D1
Craigleith Gdns	48	D1
Craigleith Gro	48	D1
Craigleith Hill	49	E1
Craigleith Hill Av	45	E6
Craigleith Hill Cres	45	E6
Craigleith Hill Gdns	45	E6
Craigleith Hill Grn	45	E6
Craigleith Hill Gro	45	E6
Craigleith Hill Loan	45	E6
Craigleith Hill Pk	45	E6
Craigleith Hill Row	45	E6
Craigleith Retail Pk	45	E6
Craigleith Ri	48	D2
Craigleith Rd	49	E1
Craigleith Vw	49	E1
Craigroyston Pl	44	B3
Cranston St	43	E2
Crarae Av	49	E2
Crawford Br 12	47	F6
Crewe Bk	45	F3
Crewe Cres	45	E3
Crewe Gro	45	F3
Crewe Loan	45	E3
Crewe Path	45	E3
Crewe Pl	45	E3
Crewe Rd Gdns	45	E3
Crewe Rd N	45	E3
Crewe Rd S	45	E4
Crewe Rd W	45	E3
Crewe Ter	45	E3
Crewe Toll	45	E4
Crichton St	43	D3
Crichton's Cl 25	43	F2
Crighton Pl	47	E5
Croall Pl	46	D6
Croft-an-righ	43	F1
Cromwell Pl	47	E2
Crown Pl	47	E4
Crown St	47	E4
Cumberland St	46	B6
Cumberland St N E La	46	B6
Cumberland St N W La	46	B6
Cumberland St S E La		
Cumberland St S W La	46	B6
Cumin Pl	50	D5
Cumlodden Av	48	D2
Cunningham Pl 4	47	E4

Name	Page	Grid
D		
Daisy Ter 3	49	F6
Dalgety Av	47	G6
Dalgety Rd	47	G6
Dalgety St	51	G1
Dalkeith Rd	43	F4
Dalmeny Rd	46	C3
Dalmeny St	47	E5
Dalry Pl	42	A3
Dalry Rd	49	G3
Dalrymple Cres	50	D6
Dalziel Pl 5	51	F1
Damside	42	A2
Dania Ct	48	A6
Danube St	42	A1
Darnaway St	42	B1
Darnell Rd	43	H3
Davidson Gdns	44	B5
Davidson Pk	45	E5
Davidson Rd	45	E5
Davie St	43	E3
Dean Bk La	46	A6
Dean Br	42	A1
Dean Pk Cres	42	A1
Dean Pk Ms	45	H6
Dean Pk St	45	H6
Dean Path	49	G1

Name	Page	Grid
Dean Path Bldgs 2	42	A2
Dean St	45	H6
Dean Ter	42	A1
Deanery Cl 11	51	H1
Deanhaugh St	46	A6
Delhaig	48	D6
Denham Grn Av	46	A3
Denham Grn Pl	46	A3
Denham Grn Ter	46	A3
Derby St	46	C2
Devon Pl	49	G3
Dewar Pl	42	A3
Dewar Pl La	42	A3
Dick Pl	50	C6
Dickson St	47	E5
Dicksonfield	46	D6
Dickson's Cl 31	43	E2
Distillery La	49	G3
Dock Pl	47	E2
Dock St	47	E2
Dorset Pl	49	H5
Douglas Cres	49	G2
Douglas Gdns	49	G2
Douglas Gdns Ms 3	49	G2
Douglas Ter 13	42	A3
Doune Ter	42	B1
Downfield Pl	49	G4
Downie Gro	48	A4
Downie Ter	48	A4
Drum Ter	47	F6
Drumdryan St	42	B4
Drummond Pl	46	B6
Drummond St	43	E3
Drumsheugh Gdns	42	A2
Drumsheugh Pl 11	42	A2
Dryden Gdns	46	D5
Dryden Pl	51	E5
Dryden St	46	D5
Dryden Ter	46	D5
Drylaw Av	44	D6
Drylaw Cres	44	C6
Drylaw Gdns	44	C5
Drylaw Grn	44	C6
Drylaw Gro	44	C6
Drylaw Ho Gdns	44	C5
Drylaw Ho Paddock	44	C5
Dublin Meuse	43	D1
Dublin St	46	C6
Dublin St La N	46	C6
Dublin St La S	43	D1
Dudley Av	46	C2
Dudley Av S	46	D3
Dudley Bk	46	C2
Dudley Cres	46	C2
Dudley Gdns	46	C2
Dudley Gro	46	C2
Dudley Ter	46	C2
Duff Rd	49	G4
Duff St	49	G4
Duff St La	49	G4
Duke Pl	47	F4
Duke St	47	F4
Duke's Wk	51	G2
Dumbiedykes Rd	43	F3
Dunbar St	42	B3
Duncan Pl	47	F4
Duncan St	50	D6
Dundas St	46	B6
Dundee St	49	G4
Dundee Ter	49	G5
Dundonald St	46	B6
Dunedin St	46	C5
Dunlop's Ct 12	42	C3
Dunrobin Pl	46	A6

Name	Page	Grid
E		
Earl Grey St	42	B3
Earl Haig Gdns	46	A3
Earl Haig Homes	48	B6
Earlston Pl	51	F1
East Adam St	43	E3
East Broughton Pl 4	46	C6

Name	Page	Grid
East Castle Rd	49	H5
East Claremont St	46	C6
East Ct 2	48	D1
East Cromwell St	47	E2
East Crosscauseway	43	E4
East Fettes Av	45	G5
East Fountainbridge	42	B3
East Hermitage Pl	47	F4
East Lillypot	46	A3
East London St	46	C6
East Mkt St	43	D2
East Mayfield	51	E6
East Montgomery Pl	47	E6
East Newington Pl	50	D5
East Norton Pl	43	F1
East Parkside	43	F4
East Preston St	50	D5
East Preston St La 3	50	D5
East Restalrig Ter	47	G4
East Sciennes St	50	D5
East Scotland St La	46	C6
East Silvermills La	46	A6
East Trinity Rd	46	A3
East Werberside	45	F4
East Werberside Pl	45	F4
Easter Belmont Rd	48	C3
Easter Dalry Dr	49	G4
Easter Dalry Pl 2	49	G3
Easter Dalry Rigg 8	49	G4
Easter Dalry Rd	49	G3
Easter Dalry Wynd	49	G3
Easter Drylaw Av	44	D5
Easter Drylaw Bk	44	D4
Easter Drylaw Dr	45	E5
Easter Drylaw Gdns	44	D5
Easter Drylaw Gro	44	D5
Easter Drylaw Loan	44	D4
Easter Drylaw Pl	44	D5
Easter Drylaw Vw	44	D5
Easter Drylaw Way	44	D5
Easter Hermitage	47	G5
Easter Rd	47	E6
Easter Warriston	46	B4
Edina Pl	47	E6
Edina St	47	E6
Edinburgh Dock	47	G2
Eglinton Cres	49	G3
Eglinton St 10	49	F3
Eildon St	46	B5
Eildon Ter	46	A5
Elbe St	47	F3
Elder St	43	D1
Elder St E 5	43	D1
Elgin Pl	49	G3
Elgin St	47	E6
Elgin St N	47	E6
Elgin Ter	47	E6
Elizafield	46	D4
Ellersly Rd	48	C3
Elliot St	47	E6
Elm Pl 2	47	G4
Elm Row	46	D6
Elmwood Ter	47	G4
Eltringham Gdns	48	D6
Eltringham Gro	48	D6
Eltringham Ter	48	D6
Esdaile Bk	50	C6
Esdaile Gdns	50	C6
Esdaile Pk 2	50	C6
Esplanade	42	C3
Eton Ter	42	A1
Ettrick Gro	49	H5
Ettrick Loan	49	G6
Ettrick Rd	49	G6
Ettrickdale Pl	46	A5
Eyre Cres	46	B6

Name	Page	Grid
Eyre Pl	46	B6
Eyre Ter	46	B6
F		
Falcon Gdns	50	A6
Ferry Rd	46	C3
Ferry Rd Av	45	E4
Ferry Rd Dr	45	E3
Ferry Rd Gdns	44	D4
Ferry Rd Gro	44	D4
Ferry Rd Pl	44	D4
Ferryfield	45	G4
Festival Sq 7	42	B3
Fettes Av	45	G6
Fettes Ri	45	G4
Fettes Row	46	B6
Fidra Ct	44	B3
Findhorn Pl	50	D5
Findlay Av	47	H5
Findlay Cotts	47	H5
Findlay Gdns	47	H5
Findlay Gro	47	H5
Findlay Medway	47	H5
Fingal Pl	50	C5
Fingzies Pl 3	47	G4
Fishmarket Sq 2	46	C1
Fleshmarket Cl 13	43	D2
Forbes Rd	50	A6
Forbes St	43	E4
Ford's Rd	48	C6
Forres St	42	B1
Forrest Hill	43	D3
Forrest Rd	43	D3
Fort Ho	46	D2
Forth Ind Est	45	F1
Forth St	43	D1
Forthview Rd	44	D6
Forthview Ter	44	C6
Fountainbridge	42	B4
Fowler Ter	49	G5
Fox St	47	G3
Fraser Av	45	H3
Fraser Cres	45	H3
Fraser Gdns	45	H3
Fraser Gro	45	H3
Frederick St	42	C1
G		
Gabriel's Rd 6	43	D1
Gabriel's Rd (Stockbridge) 17	46	A6
Gardiner Gro	44	C6
Gardiner Rd	44	C6
Gardiner Ter	48	C1
Gardner's Cres	42	A3
Garscube Ter	49	E2
Gayfield Cl	46	D6
Gayfield Pl	46	D6
Gayfield Pl La	46	D6
Gayfield Sq	46	C6
Gayfield St	46	D6
Gayfield St La	46	C6
George IV Br	43	D2
George Sq	43	D4
George Sq La	43	D4
George St	42	B2
Gibbs Entry	43	E3
Gibson St	46	D4
Gibson Ter	42	A4
Gifford Pk	43	E4
Giles St	47	E3
Gillespie Cres	42	B4
Gillespie Pl	42	B4
Gillespie St	42	B4
Gillsland Pk	49	G6
Gillsland Rd	49	G6
Gilmore Pk	42	A4
Gilmore Pl	49	H5
Gilmore Pl La	42	B4
Gilmour St	43	E3
Gilmour's Entry 7	43	E3
Gladstone Pl	47	G4
Gladstone Ter	50	D5
Glanville Pl 5	46	A6

Glen St	42	C3
Glencairn Cres	49	G3
Glendevon Av	48	C4
Glendevon Gdns	48	C4
Glendevon Gro	48	C4
Glendevon Pk	48	C5
Glendevon Pl	48	C4
Glendevon Rd	48	C5
Glendevon Ter	48	C4
Glenfinlas St	42	B2
Glengyle Ter	42	B4
Glenlea Cotts	48	D6
Glenlee Av	51	H2
Glenlee Gdns	51	H2
Glenogle Ct	46	A5
Glenogle Pl 16	46	A6
Glenogle Rd	46	A6
Glenogle Ter	46	A6
Glenorchy Pl 4	43	E1
Glenorchy Ter	51	E6
Gloucester La	42	B1
Gloucester Pl	42	B1
Gloucester Sq	42	B1
Gloucester St	42	B1
Goldenacre Ter	46	A4
Gordon St	47	F4
Gorgie Cotts	48	D6
Gorgie Pk Cl	49	E6
Gorgie Pk Rd	49	E5
Gorgie Rd	49	E5
Gosford Pl	46	C3
Graham St	46	D3
Grandfield	46	B3
Grandville	46	B2
Grange Ct	50	D5
Grange Cres	50	C6
Grange Loan	50	B6
Grange Loan Gdns	50	C6
Grange Rd	50	C5
Granton Cres	45	G2
Granton Gdns	45	G2
Granton Gro	45	G2
Granton Mains Av	44	D2
Granton Mains Bk 1	44	D2
Granton Mains Brae	44	D2
Granton Mains Ct	45	E2
Granton Mains E	45	E2
Granton Mains Gait	44	D2
Granton Mains Vale	44	D2
Granton Mains Wynd	44	D2
Granton Medway	45	F2
Granton Mill Cres	44	D2
Granton Mill Dr	44	D2
Granton Mill March	44	C3
Granton Mill Pk	44	C3
Granton Mill Pl	44	C2
Granton Mill Rd	44	C2
Granton Mill W 1	44	C2
Granton Pk Av	45	F1
Granton Pl	45	G2
Granton Rd	45	G2
Granton Sq	45	G1
Granton Ter	45	G2
Granton Vw	45	G1
Grantully Pl	51	E6
Granville Ter	49	H5
Grassmarket	42	C3
Grays Ct 6	43	E3
Gray's Loan	49	F6
Great Junct St	47	E3
Great King St	42	C1
Great Michael Cl 7	46	C1
Great Michael Ri	46	C2
Great Michael Sq 1	46	C1
Great Stuart St	42	A2
Green, The	44	A4
Green St	46	C6
Greendale Pk	44	B4
Greenhill Ct	50	A5
Greenhill Gdns	50	A5
Greenhill Pk	50	A6
Greenhill Pl	50	A6
Greenhill Ter	50	A5
Greenside End 12	43	E1
Greenside La	43	E1
Greenside Pl 11	43	E1
Greenside Row	43	E1
Greyfriars Pl	43	D3
Grierson Av	45	H2
Grierson Cres	45	H2
Grierson Gdns	45	H2
Grierson Rd	45	G2
Grierson Sq	45	H2
Grierson Vil	45	H2
Grigor Av	45	E5
Grigor Dr	45	E5
Grigor Gdns	45	E5
Grigor Ter	45	E5
Grindlay St	42	B3
Grindlay St Ct	42	B3
Groathill Av	44	D6
Groathill Gdns E	44	D6
Groathill Gdns W	44	D6
Groathill Rd N	44	D5
Groathill Rd S	44	D6
Grosvenor Cres	49	G3
Grosvenor Gdns	49	G3
Grosvenor St	42	A3
Grove St	42	A3
Grove Ter 4	42	A3
Guardianswood	48	D3
Gullan's Cl	43	E2
Gunnet Ct	44	B3
Guthrie St	43	D3
Gypsy Brae	44	D2

H

Haddington Pl	46	D6
Haddon's Ct	43	E3
Hailes St	42	B4
Halmyre St	47	E5
Hamburgh Pl 6	46	D2
Hamilton Pl	46	A6
Hamilton Wynd	46	D2
Hamilton's Folly Ms 5	43	E4
Hammermen's Entry	43	E2
Hampton Pl 4	49	F3
Hampton Ter	49	F3
Hanover St	42	C1
Harden Pl	49	G5
Hardwell Cl	43	E4
Harrismith Pl	47	F6
Harrison Gdns	49	F6
Harrison La	49	G5
Harrison Pl	49	F6
Harrison Rd	49	F5
Hart St	46	C6
Hart St La	46	C6
Hartington Gdns	50	A5
Hartington Pl	49	H5
Hatton Pl	50	C5
Haugh St	46	A6
Hawkhill	47	G5
Hawkhill Av	47	F5
Hawkhill Ct	47	G5
Hawthorn Bldgs 5	49	G2
Hawthorn Ter 5	42	A2
Hawthornbank La	42	A2
Hawthornbank Pl	46	D2
Hawthornbank Ter 20	46	D2
Hawthornden Pl	46	D5
Hawthornvale	46	C2
Haymarket	42	A3
Haymarket Ter	49	G3
Haymarket Yards	49	G3
Hazelbank Ter	49	F6
Henderland Rd	49	E3
Henderson Gdns 4	47	E3
Henderson Pl	46	B6
Henderson Pl La	46	A6
Henderson Row	46	A6
Henderson St	47	E3
Henderson Ter	49	G5
Henry Pl	43	F4
Henry St	43	F4
Heriot Br	42	C3
Heriot Cross 17	42	C3
Heriot Hill Ter	46	B5
Heriot Pl	42	C3
Heriot Row	42	B1
Hermand Cres	49	F6
Hermand St	49	E6
Hermand Ter	49	E6
Hermitage Pk	47	G5
Hermitage Pk Gro	47	G5
Hermitage Pk Lea	47	G5
Hermitage Pk S	47	G5
Hermitage Pl	47	F4
Hermits Cft	43	F4
High Riggs	42	C3
High Sch Yards	43	E3
High St	43	D2
Hill Pl	43	E3
Hill Sq	43	E3
Hill St	42	B1
Hill St La N	42	B1
Hill St La S	42	C2
Hillend Pl 10	51	H1
Hillhouse Rd	44	A5
Hillpark Av	44	A5
Hillpark Brae	48	A1
Hillpark Ct	44	A5
Hillpark Cres	44	A6
Hillpark Dr	44	A5
Hillpark Gdns	44	A6
Hillpark Grn	44	A6
Hillpark Gro	44	A6
Hillpark Loan	44	B6
Hillpark Rd	44	A6
Hillpark Ter	44	A6
Hillpark Way	44	B6
Hillpark Wd	44	B6
Hillside Cres	46	D6
Hillside St	47	E6
Hillview	46	A5
Hollybank Ter	49	F6
Holyrood Ct	43	F2
Holyrood Pk	51	F2
Holyrood Pk Rd	51	E5
Holyrood Rd	43	E2
Home St	42	B4
Hope Pk Cres	43	E4
Hope Pk Sq 1	43	E4
Hope Pk Ter	43	E4
Hope St	42	B2
Hope St La	42	B2
Hope Ter	50	B6
Hopefield Ter	46	D2
Hopetoun Cres	46	D6
Hopetoun St	46	D6
Horne Ter	42	A4
Horse Wynd	43	F2
House o'Hill Av	44	B5
House o'Hill Brae	44	B5
House o'Hill Cres	44	B5
House o'Hill Gdns	44	B5
House o'Hill Grn	44	B5
House o'Hill Gro	44	B5
House o'Hill Pl	44	B5
House o'Hill Rd	44	C5
House o'Hill Row	44	C5
House o'Hill Ter	44	C6
Howard Pl	46	B5
Howard St	46	B5
Howden St	43	E3
Howe St	42	C1
Hugh Miller Pl	46	A6
Hunter Sq	43	D2
Hunter's Cl 43	43	D2
Huntingdon Pl	46	D6
Huntly St	46	B5
Hutchison Crossway	49	E3
Hutchison Ho	49	E6
Hutchison Medway	49	E6
Hutchison Pk	48	D6
Hutchison Rd	49	E6
Hutchison Vw	48	D6
Hutton Cl	43	F2
Hutton Rd	43	F2

I

Imperial Dock	47	F1
Inchcolm Ct	44	D3
Inchgarvie Ct	45	E4
Inchkeith Ct	46	D5
Inchmickery Ct	44	B3
India Bldgs 18	43	D3
India Pl	42	B1
India St	42	B1
Industrial Rd	47	F4
Industry Home 7	46	D3
Industry La	46	D3
Infirmary St	43	E3
Inglis Ct 19	42	C3
Inverleith Av	46	A4
Inverleith Av S	46	A4
Inverleith Gdns	45	H4
Inverleith Gro	45	G5
Inverleith Pl	45	H4
Inverleith Pl La	46	A4
Inverleith Row	46	A4
Inverleith Ter	46	A5
Inverleith Ter La	46	A5
Iona St	47	E5
Ivy Ter	49	F5

J

Jamaica Ms	42	B1
Jamaica St	42	B1
Jamaica St N La	42	B1
Jamaica St S La	42	B1
Jamaica St W 15	42	B1
James' Ct 20	43	D2
James Craig Wk	43	D1
Jameson Pl	47	E5
Jane St	47	E4
Jane Ter 8	51	F1
Jawbone Wk	43	D4
Jeffrey Av	48	C1
Jeffrey St	43	D2
Jessfield Ter	46	C2
John Cotton Business Cen	47	F6
John's La	47	F3
John's Pl	47	F4
Johnston Ter	42	C3
Junction Pl	47	E4

K

Keir St	42	C3
Keith Cres	48	C1
Keith Row	48	D1
Keith Ter	48	C1
Kemp Pl	46	A6
Kenmure Av	51	H2
Kerr St	46	A6
Kew Ter	49	F3
Kilgraston Ct	50	B6
Kilgraston Rd	50	C6
Kilmaurs Rd	51	F6
Kilmaurs Ter	51	F6
Kincaid's Ct	43	D3
Kinellan Gdns	48	D3
Kinellan Rd	48	D2
King St	47	E3
Kinghorn Pl	46	C3
King's Br	42	C3
Kings Haugh	51	H6
King's Meadow	51	H5
King's Stables La	42	C3
King's Stables Rd	42	C3
Kingsburgh Rd	48	D3
Kinnear Rd	45	G4
Kirk St	47	E4
Kirkgate	47	F3
Kirkhill Dr	51	F6
Kirkhill Gdns	51	F5
Kirkhill Rd	51	F5
Kirkhill Ter	51	F5
Kirkwood Pl 9	51	F1
Kittle Yards	50	D5
Kyle Pl	43	F1

L

Ladehead	46	C4
Lady Lawson St	42	C3
Lady Menzies Pl	51	F1
Lady Stair's Cl 6	43	D2
Lady Wynd	42	C3
Lamb's Cl 2	43	E4
Lamb's Ct 8	46	B1
Lansdowne Cres	49	G3
Lapicide Pl	46	D3
Largo Pl	46	D3
Lauder Loan	50	D6
Lauder Rd	50	C6
Lauderdale St	50	B5
Laurel Ter 6	49	F5
Laurie St	47	F4
Lauriston Gdns	42	C3
Lauriston Pk	42	C3
Lauriston Pl	42	B4
Lauriston St	42	C3
Lauriston Ter	42	C3
Laverockbank Av	46	B2
Laverockbank Cres	46	B2
Laverockbank Gdns	46	B2
Laverockbank Gro	46	B2
Laverockbank Rd	46	B2
Laverockbank Ter	46	B2
Lawnmarket	43	D2
Leamington Pl	42	B4
Leamington Rd	42	A4
Leamington Ter	42	B4
Learmonth Av	45	G6
Learmonth Ct	49	G1
Learmonth Cres	49	G1
Learmonth Gdns	49	G1
Learmonth Gdns La	49	G1
Learmonth Gdns Ms	45	H6
Learmonth Gro	45	G6
Learmonth Pk	45	G6
Learmonth Pl	45	G6
Learmonth Ter	49	G1
Learmonth Ter La	49	G1
Learmonth Vw 7	42	A1
Leith Docks	47	E1
Leith Links	47	F4
Leith St	43	D1
Leith Wk	46	D6
Lennel Av	48	D2
Lennox Row	46	A2
Lennox St	42	A1
Lennox St La	42	A1
Leopold Pl	46	D6
Leslie Pl	45	H6
Leven Cl 4	42	B4
Leven St	42	B4
Leven Ter	42	B4
Lewis Ter 12	42	A3
Liddesdale Pl	46	A6
Lily Ter 1	49	F6
Lilyhill Ter	51	H1
Limes, The	50	D6
Lindean Pl	47	G4
Lindsay Pl	46	D2
Lindsay Rd	46	D2
Lindsay St	46	D2
Links Gdns	47	G3
Links Gdns La	47	G3
Links La 9	47	F3
Links Pl	47	F3
Linksview Ho	47	F3
Lismore Av	51	H1
Lismore Cres	51	H1
Little King St	43	D1

Livingstone Pl 50 C5
Lixmount Av 46 B2
Lixmount Gdns 46 B2
Loaning Rd 47 H6
Loch Rd 44 B6
Lochend Av 47 G6
Lochend Castle 47 G6
Barns
Lochend Cl 43 F2
Lochend Cres 47 H6
Lochend Dr 47 G6
Lochend Gdns 47 G6
Lochend Gro 47 H6
Lochend Pk 47 H6
Lochend Quad 47 H6
Lochend Rd 47 G6
Lochend Rd S 47 G6
Lochend Sq 47 G6
Lochrin Bldgs 42 B4
Lochrin Pl 42 B4
Lochrin Ter 5 42 B4
Lochview Ct 43 F2
Logan St 46 B6
Loganlea Dr 51 H1
Loganlea Gdns 47 H6
Logie Grn Gdns 46 B5
Logie Grn Loan 46 B5
Logie Grn Rd 46 B5
Logie Mill 46 B5
Lomond Rd 46 A2
London Rd 43 E1
London St 46 C6
Long Craig Rigg 44 D1
Long Craig Rd 44 D1
Lonsdale Ter 42 C4
Lord Russell Pl 6 50 D5
Lorne Pl 47 E5
Lorne Sq 47 E5
Lorne St 47 E5
Lothian Rd 42 B2
Lothian St 43 D3
Lovers' Loan 50 C5
Lower Gilmore Pl 42 A4
Lower Granton Rd 46 A2
Lower London Rd 51 F1
Lufra Bk 45 H2
Lutton Pl 43 E4
Lyne St 51 F1
Lynedoch Pl 42 A2
Lynedoch Pl La 42 A2

M
Mackenzie Pl 42 B1
Madeira Pl 46 D3
Madeira St 46 D2
Magdala Cres 49 G3
Magdala Ms 49 G3
Maidencraig Ct 44 D6
Maidencraig Cres 44 D6
Maidencraig Gro 44 D6
Main Pt 42 C3
Main St 44 A5
Malta Grn 8 46 A6
Malta Ter 46 A6
Manderston St 47 E4
Manor Pl 42 A2
Mansfield Pl 46 C6
Mansionhouse Rd 50 C5
March Gait 44 A6
March Gro 44 A6
March Pines 44 A6
March Rd 44 A6
Marchfield Gro 44 B5
Marchfield Pk 44 A5
Marchfield Pk La 44 A5
Marchfield Ter 44 B6
Marchhall Cres 51 F5
Marchhall Pl 51 F5
Marchhall Rd 51 F5
Marchmont Cres 50 B5
Marchmont Rd 50 B5
Marchmont St 50 B5
Mardale Cres 49 H6
Marine Dr 44 B2
Marine Esplanade 47 H3

Marionville Av 47 G6
Marionville Cres 47 H6
Marionville Dr 47 H6
Marionville Gro 47 H6
Marionville 47 H6
Medway 1
Marionville Pk 47 G6
Marionville Rd 51 F1
Marischal Pl 1 48 D1
Maritime La 47 F3
Maritime St 47 F3
Market St 43 D2
Marshall St 23 43 E3
Marshall's Ct 9 43 E1
Martello Ct 44 B3
Maryfield 43 F1
Maryfield Pl 51 F1
Mary's Pl 9 45 H6
May Ct 44 B3
Mayfield Gdns 51 E6
Mayfield Gdns La 51 E6
Mayfield Rd 51 E6
Mayfield Ter 51 E6
Mayville Gdns 46 B2
Mayville Gdns E 46 B2
McDonald Pl 46 C5
McDonald Rd 46 C5
McDonald St 46 D5
McKelvie Par 46 A1
McLaren Rd 51 F6
McLaren Ter 20 42 A3
McLeod St 49 F4
McNeill St 42 A4
Meadow Bk 47 F6
Shop Pk
Meadow La 43 D4
Meadow Pl 42 C4
Meadow Pl La 50 C5
Meadowbank 51 G1
Meadowbank Av 51 G1
Meadowbank Cres 51 G1
Meadowbank Ho 51 H1
Meadowbank Pl 7 51 H1
Meadowbank Ter 51 G1
Melbourne Pl 24 43 D2
Melgund Ter 46 C6
Melville Cres 42 A2
Melville Dr 42 C4
Melville Pl 6 42 A2
Melville St 42 A2
Melville St La 42 A2
Melville Ter 50 C5
Mentone Gdns 51 E6
Merchant St 43 D3
Merchiston Av 49 H5
Merchiston Bk Av 49 H6
Merchiston Bk 49 H6
Gdns
Merchiston Cres 49 H6
Merchiston Gro 49 F5
Merchiston Ms 49 H5
Merchiston Pk 49 H5
Merchiston Pl 49 H6
Mertoun Pl 49 G5
Meuse La 43 D2
Mid Gillsland Rd 49 G6
Middle 43 D4
Meadow Wk
Middle Pier 45 G1
Middleby St 51 E6
Middlefield 46 D5
Mill La 47 E3
Miller Row 42 A2
Millerfield Pl 50 C5
Milnacre 46 C4
Milton St 51 F1
Minto St 51 E5
Mitchell St 47 F3
Moat Dr 49 E6
Moat Ho 49 E6
Moat Pl 49 E6
Moat St 49 E6
Moat Ter 49 E6
Moncrieff Ter 50 D5
Monkwood Ct 50 C6
Monmouth Ter 46 A3

Montagu Ter 46 A4
Montague St 43 E4
Montgomery St 46 D6
Montgomery St La 46 D6
Montpelier 49 H5
Montpelier Pk 49 H5
Montpelier Ter 49 H5
Montrose Ter 43 F1
Moray Pk 51 F1
Moray Pk Ter 51 F1
Moray Pl 42 B1
Morningside Rd 49 H6
Morrison Circ 42 A3
Morrison Cres 42 A3
Morrison Link 42 A3
Morrison St 42 A3
Moston Ter 51 E6
Mound, The 42 C2
Mound Pl 42 C2
Mount Gra 50 B6
Muirdale Ter 1 44 C6
Muirhouse Av 44 C4
Muirhouse Av N 44 C3
Muirhouse Bk 44 C4
Muirhouse Cl 44 B4
Muirhouse Ct 44 C3
Muirhouse Cres 44 C3
Muirhouse Dr 44 B3
Muirhouse Gdns 44 B3
Muirhouse Grn 44 C4
Muirhouse Gro 44 B3
Muirhouse Loan 44 C3
Muirhouse 44 B3
Medway
Muirhouse Pk 44 B4
Muirhouse 44 C3
Parkway
Muirhouse Pl E 44 C4
Muirhouse Pl W 44 C4
Muirhouse Ter 44 B4
Muirhouse Vw 44 C3
Muirhouse Way 44 C4
Mulberry Pl 46 C3
Munro Pl 1 46 B5
Murano Pl 47 E6
Murdoch Ter 42 A4
Murieston Cres 49 F4
Murieston Cres 49 G4
La 7
Murieston La 49 F4
Murieston Pl 49 F4
Murieston Rd 49 F4
Murieston Ter 49 F4
Murrayfield Av 49 E3
Murrayfield Dr 49 E3
Murrayfield Gdns 49 E2
Murrayfield Pl 1 49 E3
Murrayfield Rd 48 D2
Myrtle Ter 49 F5

N
Napier Loan 49 G6
Napier Rd 49 G6
Nelson Pl 10 42 C1
Nelson St 42 C1
Nether Craigwell 43 F1
Netherby Rd 45 H3
New Arthur Pl 43 E3
New Arthur St 29 43 E3
New Bells Ct 4 47 F3
New Broompark 45 F1
New Broughton 46 C6
New Cut Rigg 46 C3
New John's Pl 43 E4
New La 46 C2
New Orchardfield 47 E4
New Skinner's Cl 43 E2
New St 43 E2
Newbattle Ter 50 A6
Newhaven 46 B1
Main St
Newhaven Pl 46 C1
Newhaven Rd 46 D4
Newington Rd 50 D5
Newkirkgate 5 47 E4

Newlands Pk 51 E6
News Steps 43 D2
Newton St 49 F5
Nicholfield 46 C2
Nicolson Sq 43 D3
Nicolson St 43 E3
Niddry St 43 D2
Niddry St S 26 43 E3
Nisbet Ct 47 G5
Noble Pl 47 G4
North Bk St 43 D2
North Br 43 D2
North Br Arc 42 43 D2
North Castle St 42 B1
North Charlotte St 42 B1
North Clyde St 43 D1
La 11
North E Circ Pl 42 B1
North Fort St 46 D2
North 46 D2
Hillhousefield
North Junct St 46 D2
North Leith Mill 19 46 D2
North Leith Sands 46 D2
North Meadow 42 C4
Wk
North Pk Ter 45 H6
North Richmond 43 E3
St 10
North St. Andrew 43 D1
La
North St. Andrew 43 D1
St
North St. David St 43 D1
North Werber Pk 45 F5
North Werber Pl 45 F4
North Werber Rd 45 F5
North W Circ Pl 42 B1
Northcote St 49 G4
Northumberland 42 C1
Pl La
Northumberland 42 C1
St
Northumberland 42 C1
St N E La
Northumberland 42 C1
St N W La
Northumberland 42 C1
St S E La
Northumberland 42 C1
St S W La
Northview Ct 44 C3
Norton Pk 47 F6
Nottingham Pl 43 E1

O
Oakfield Pl 43 E3
Oakville Ter 47 G4
Ocean Dr 47 E2
Ocean Terminal 46 D1
Shop Cen
Ogilvie Ter 49 F6
Old Assembly 43 D2
Cl 27
Old Broughton 13 46 C6
Old Ch La 51 E6
Old Fishmarket Cl 43 D2
Old Tolbooth 43 E2
Wynd
Orchard Bk 49 F1
Orchard Brae 45 G6
Orchard Brae Av 49 F1
Orchard Brae 49 F1
Gdns
Orchard Brae 49 F1
Gdns W
Orchard Brae W 45 G6
Orchard Cres 49 E1
Orchard Dr 49 E1
Orchard Gro 45 G6
Orchard Pl 45 F6
Orchard Rd 49 E1
Orchard Rd S 49 E1
Orchard Ter 49 F1

Orchard Toll 49 F1
Orchardfield La 47 E5
Ormidale Ter 48 D3
Orwell Pl 49 G4
Orwell Ter 49 G4
Osborne Ter 49 G3
Oxcars Ct 44 B3
Oxcraig St 45 G1
Oxford St 43 F4
Oxford Ter 42 A1

P
Paisley Cres 51 H2
Paisley Gdns 51 H2
Paisley Ter 51 H2
Palmerston Pl 42 A2
Palmerston Pl La 42 A3
Palmerston Rd 50 C5
Panmure Pl 42 C4
Pape's Cotts 49 E3
Park Pl 46 B2
Park Rd 46 B2
Parkside St 43 F4
Parkside Ter 43 F4
Parkvale Pl 47 G4
Parliament Sq 43 D2
Parliament St 47 F3
Parsons Grn Ter 2 51 H1
Patrick Geddes 42 C3
Steps 44
Patriothall 10 46 A6
Pattison St 47 F3
Peacock Ct 46 C1
Peel Ter 51 E6
Pembroke Pl 49 F3
Pennywell Cotts 44 C2
Pennywell Ct 44 C2
Pennywell Gdns 44 B3
Pennywell Gro 44 C3
Pennywell 44 C3
Medway
Pennywell Pl 44 C3
Pennywell Rd 44 C3
Pennywell Vil 44 C2
Persevere Ct 47 E2
Perth St 46 A6
Picardy Pl 43 E1
Pier Pl 46 B1
Piershill La 3 51 H1
Piershill Pl 4 51 H1
Piershill Sq W 51 H1
Pilrig Cotts 47 E5
Pilrig Gdns 46 D4
Pilrig Glebe 47 E5
Pilrig Ho Cl 46 D4
Pilrig Ind Est 46 D4
Pilrig Pl 47 E5
Pilrig St 46 D4
Pilton Av 45 E3
Pilton Cres 45 G3
Pilton Dr 45 F3
Pilton Dr N 45 F2
Pilton Gdns 45 G3
Pilton Loan 45 F3
Pilton Pk 45 F3
Pilton Pl 45 F3
Pinkhill 48 A4
Pirniefield Bk 47 H4
Pirniefield Gdns 47 H4
Pirniefield Gro 47 H4
Pirniefield Pl 47 H4
Pirniefield Ter 47 H4
Pirrie St 47 E4
Pitlochry Pl 47 F6
Pitsligo Rd 50 A6
Pitt St 46 C3
Playfair Steps 29 42 C2
Pleasance 43 E3
Polwarth Cres 49 H5
Polwarth Gdns 49 G5
Polwarth Gro 49 G6
Polwarth Pk 49 G5
Polwarth Pl 49 G5
Polwarth Ter 49 G6
Ponton St 42 B4

Poplar La	47	F3
Port Hamilton	42	B3
Porterfield Rd	45	F5
Portgower Pl	45	H6
Portland Pl 9	46	D2
Portland St	46	D2
Portland Ter 10	46	D2
Portsburgh Sq 30	42	C3
Potterrow	43	D3
Powderhall Rd	46	C5
Prestonfield Av	51	F6
Prestonfield Bk	51	F6
Prestonfield Cres	51	F6
Prestonfield Gdns	51	F6
Prestonfield Rd	51	F6
Prestonfield Ter	51	F6
Priestfield Av	51	G6
Priestfield Cres	51	G6
Priestfield Gdns	51	G6
Priestfield Gro	51	F5
Priestfield Rd	51	F6
Priestfield Rd N	51	F5
Primrose Bk Rd	46	A2
Primrose St	47	F4
Primrose Ter	49	F5
Prince of Wales Dock	47	E1
Prince Regent St	47	E1
Princes Mall	43	D2
Princes St	42	C2
Prospect Bk Cres	47	G5
Prospect Bk Gdns	47	G5
Prospect Bk Gro	47	H4
Prospect Bk Pl	47	H4
Prospect Bk Rd	47	G4
Prospect Bk Ter	47	H4

Q

Quality St	44	A5
Quality St La	44	A5
Quarry Cl	43	E4
Quayside Mills 3	47	E3
Quayside St	47	E3
Queen Charlotte La	47	F3
Queen Charlotte St	47	F3
Queen St	42	B1
Queen St Gdns E	42	C1
Queen St Gdns W	42	C1
Queen's Av	44	C6
Queen's Av S	44	D6
Queen's Cres	51	E6
Queen's Dr	43	F3
Queen's Gdns	44	C6
Queen's Pk Av	51	G1
Queen's Pk Ct	51	H2
Queen's Rd	44	D6
Queensferry Rd	49	G1
Queensferry St	42	A2
Queensferry St La	42	A2
Queensferry Ter	49	F1
Quilts, The	46	D3
Quilts Wynd	46	D3

R

Raeburn Ms	45	H6
Raeburn Pl	45	H6
Raeburn St	45	H6
Ramsay Gdn	42	C2
Ramsay La	42	C2
Randolph Cliff	42	A2
Randolph Cres	42	A2
Randolph La	42	B2
Randolph Pl	42	B2
Rankeillor St	43	E4
Ratcliffe Ter	50	D5
Ravelston Ct	49	E2
Ravelston Dykes	49	E2
Ravelston Dykes La	48	B2
Ravelston Dykes Rd	48	C1
Ravelston Gdn	48	D2

Ravelston Hts	48	D1
Ravelston Ho Gro	48	D1
Ravelston Ho Loan	48	D1
Ravelston Ho Pk	48	D1
Ravelston Ho Rd	48	D1
Ravelston Pk	49	F2
Ravelston Pl 6	49	G2
Ravelston Ri	48	D2
Ravelston Ter	49	G1
Redbraes Gro	46	C4
Redbraes Pl	46	C4
Reekie's Ct	43	E3
Regent Br 14	43	D1
Regent Pl	51	F1
Regent Rd	43	E1
Regent Ter	43	E1
Regent Ter Ms	43	F1
Regent's Ct 5	49	G4
Register Pl	43	D1
Reid Ter	45	H6
Reid's Cl	43	F2
Reid's Ct 11	43	F2
Rennie's Isle	47	E2
Restalrig Av	51	H1
Restalrig Circ	47	H5
Restalrig Cres	47	H5
Restalrig Dr	47	H6
Restalrig Gdns	47	H6
Restalrig Pk	47	G5
Restalrig Rd	47	G4
Restalrig Rd S	51	H1
Restalrig Sq	47	H5
Restalrig Ter	47	F4
Richmond La	43	E3
Richmond Pl	43	E3
Richmond Ter	42	A3
Riego St	42	B3
Rillbank Cres	50	C5
Rillbank Ter	50	C5
Rintoul Pl	46	A6
Ritchie Pl	49	G5
Riversdale Cres	48	D4
Riversdale Gro	48	D3
Riversdale Rd	48	C3
Robb's Loan	48	D6
Robb's Loan Gro	48	D6
Robertson Av	49	E5
Robertson's Cl	43	E3
Robertson's Ct 17	43	F2
Rocheid Pk	45	G4
Rocheid Path	46	A5
Rochester Ter	49	H6
Rodney Pl	46	B6
Rodney St	46	B5
Romero Pl	51	E5
Ronaldson's Wf	47	E3
Rose Pk	46	A3
Rose St	42	B2
Rose St N La	42	B2
Rose St S La	42	B2
Rosebank Cotts	42	A3
Rosebank Gdns	45	H3
Rosebank Gro	45	H3
Rosebank Rd	45	H3
Rosebery Cres	49	G3
Rosebery Cres La	49	G3
Roseburn Av	49	E3
Roseburn Cliff	49	E3
Roseburn Cres	49	E4
Roseburn Dr	49	E3
Roseburn Gdns 2	49	E3
Roseburn Maltings	49	F3
Roseburn Pl	49	E3
Roseburn St	49	E4
Roseburn Ter	49	E3
Rosemount Bldgs	42	A3
Roseneath Pl	50	B5
Roseneath St	50	C5
Roseneath Ter 5	50	C5
Rosevale Pl 5	47	G4
Rosevale Ter	47	F4
Roseville Gdns	46	B2
Rossie Pl	47	E6
Rosslyn Cres	46	D5
Rosslyn Ter	46	D5

Rothesay Ms	49	G2
Rothesay Pl	49	G2
Rothesay Ter	49	G2
Roxburgh Pl	43	E3
Roxburgh St	43	E3
Royal Circ	42	B1
Royal Cres	46	B6
Royal Pk Pl	51	G1
Royal Pk Ter	51	G1
Royal Ter	43	E1
Royal Ter Ms	43	F1
Royston Mains Av	45	E2
Royston Mains Cl	45	E2
Royston Mains Cres	45	E2
Royston Mains Gdns	45	F2
Royston Mains Grn	45	F2
Royston Mains Pl	45	E2
Royston Mains Rd	45	F2
Royston Mains St	45	E2
Royston Ter	46	A4
Russell Gdns	49	F3
Russell Pl	46	A2
Russell Rd	49	F3
Rutland Ct 22	42	B3
Rutland Ct La	42	B3
Rutland Pl 8	42	B2
Rutland Sq	42	B2
Rutland St	42	B2
Ryehill Av	47	G4
Ryehill Gdns	47	G4
Ryehill Gro	47	G5
Ryehill Pl	47	G4
Ryehill Ter	47	G4

S

St. Andrew Pl	47	F4
St. Andrew Sq	43	D1
St. Anthony La	47	E3
St. Anthony Pl 14	47	E3
St. Anthony Pl 15	47	E3
St. Bernard's Cres	42	A1
St. Bernard's Row	46	A6
St. Catherine's Gdns	48	B4
St. Catherine's Pl	50	D5
St. Clair Av	47	F5
St. Clair Pl	47	F5
St. Clair Rd	47	F5
St. Clair St	47	F5
St. Colme St	42	B2
St. David's Pl 9	42	A3
St. David's Ter 10	42	A3
St. Giles' St	43	D2
St. James Cen	43	D1
St. James' Pl	43	D1
St. James Sq	43	D1
St. John St	43	E2
St. John's Cres	48	A4
St. John's Hill 9	43	E3
St. Leonard's Bk	43	F4
St. Leonard's Crag 4	43	F4
St. Leonard's Hill	43	E4
St. Leonard's La	43	E4
St. Leonard's St	43	E4
St. Margaret's Pl	50	B6
St. Margaret's Rd	50	A6
St. Mary's St	43	E2
St. Ninian's Row 18	43	D1
St. Patrick Sq	43	E4
St. Patrick St 7	43	E4
St. Peter's Bldgs	42	A4
St. Peter's Pl	42	A4
St. Stephen Pl	46	A6
St. Stephen St	46	A6
St. Teresa Pl	49	G6
St. Thomas Rd	50	C6
St. Vincent St	46	B6
Salamander Pl	47	G3
Salamander St	47	F3
Salamander Yards	47	H4

Salisbury Pl	50	D5
Salisbury Rd	51	E5
Salmond Pl	47	F6
Salvesen Cres	44	B3
Salvesen Gdns	44	C2
Salvesen Gro	44	C2
Salvesen Ter	44	C2
Sand Port	47	F2
Sandport Pl	47	E2
Sandport St	47	E2
Sauchiebank	49	F4
Saughton Av	48	D6
Saughton Cres	48	C4
Saughton Gdns	48	C4
Saughton Gro	48	C4
Saughton Loan	48	C4
Saughton Mains Av	48	A6
Saughton Mains Bk	48	A6
Saughton Mains Pk	48	A6
Saughton Mains St	48	A6
Saughton Mains Ter	48	A6
Saughton Pk	48	C4
Saughton Rd	48	A6
Saughtonhall Av	48	C4
Saughtonhall Av W	48	C4
Saughtonhall Circ	48	D4
Saughtonhall Cres	48	D4
Saughtonhall Dr	48	C3
Saughtonhall Gdns	48	D4
Saughtonhall Gro	48	D4
Saughtonhall Pl	48	D4
Saughtonhall Ter	48	D4
Saunders St	42	B1
Saxe Coburg St	46	A6
Saxe-Coburg Pl	46	A6
Saxe-Coburg Ter 12	46	A6
Sciennes	50	D5
Sciennes Gdns	50	D5
Sciennes Hill Pl	50	D5
Sciennes Ho Pl	50	D5
Sciennes Pl 9	50	D5
Sciennes Rd	50	C5
Scone Gdns	51	H1
Scotland St	46	B6
Seacot 1	47	H4
Seafield Av	47	H4
Seafield Pl	47	H4
Seafield Rd	47	H4
Seaforth Dr	44	D6
Seaforth Ter	44	D6
Sealcarr St	45	F1
Seaport St 5	47	F3
Semple St	42	B3
Seton Pl	50	D5
Shaftesbury Pk	49	F6
Shandon Cres	49	F6
Shandon Pl	49	F6
Shandon Rd	49	F6
Shandon St	49	F6
Shandon Ter	49	F6
Shandwick Pl	42	A3
Shaw's Pl	46	D6
Shaw's Sq 7	46	D6
Shaw's St	46	D5
Shaw's Ter	46	D5
Sheriff Bk	47	E3
Sheriff Brae	47	E3
Sheriff Pk	47	E3
Shore	47	F3
Shore Pl	47	F3
Shrub Pl	46	D5
Shrub Pl La	46	D5
Sienna Gdns	50	D5
Silverknowes Bk	44	A4
Silverknowes Brae	44	A4
Silverknowes Ct	44	A4
Silverknowes Cres	44	A3
Silverknowes Dell	44	B4

Silverknowes Dr	44	A4
Silverknowes Eastway	44	A4
Silverknowes Gdns	44	A3
Silverknowes Grn	44	B4
Silverknowes Gro	44	A3
Silverknowes Hill	44	A4
Silverknowes Midway	44	B4
Silverknowes Neuk	44	B5
Silverknowes Parkway	44	A3
Silverknowes Pl	44	A3
Silverknowes Rd	44	A3
Silverknowes Rd E	44	A4
Silverknowes Rd S	44	A5
Silverknowes Southway	44	B4
Silverknowes Vw	44	B4
Silvermills	46	A6
Simon Sq 4	43	E3
Sinclair Cl 2	49	F6
Sinclair Gdns	49	F5
Sinclair Pl	49	E5
Slateford Rd	49	E6
Slateford Rd Br	49	F6
Slater's Steps 26	43	F2
Sleigh Dr	47	H6
Sleigh Gdns	47	H6
Sloan St	47	E5
Smithfield St	49	E5
Smith's Pl	47	E4
Solicitor's Bldgs 33	43	D3
Somerset Pl	47	F4
South Beechwood	48	B4
South Br	43	D2
South Charlotte St	42	B2
South Clerk St	43	E4
South College St	43	D3
South E Circ Pl 13	42	B1
South Ettrick Rd	49	G6
South Fort St	46	D3
South Gayfield La	46	D6
South Gillsland Rd	49	G6
South Gray St	51	E6
South Gray's Cl	43	E2
South Groathill Av	44	D6
South Lauder Rd	50	D6
South Laverockbank Av	46	B2
South Learmonth Av	49	G1
South Learmonth Gdns	49	G1
South Lorne Pl	47	E5
South Meadow Wk	42	C4
South Oxford St	51	E5
South Pk	46	C2
South St. Andrew St	43	D1
South St. David St	43	D1
South Sloan St	47	E5
South Trinity Rd	46	A3
Spence St	51	E5
Spencer Pl	46	A2
Spey St	46	D5
Spey St La	46	D5
Spey Ter	46	D5
Spier's Pl 16	47	E3
Spittal St	42	B3
Spittal St La 21	42	C3
Spittalfield Cres	43	E4
Spottiswoode Rd	50	B5
Spottiswoode St	50	B5
Spring Gdns	51	F1
Springfield	47	E4
Springfield Bldgs 3	47	E4
Springfield La	47	E4
Springfield St	47	E4

Springwell Pl	49 G4	Thirlestane Rd	50 B5
Spylaw Rd	49 G6	Thistle Ct **15**	42 C1
Stafford St	42 A2	Thistle Pl	42 A4
Stair Pk	48 D3	Thistle St	42 C1
Stanhope Pl	49 F3	Thistle St N E La	42 C1
Stanhope St	49 F3	Thistle St N W La	42 C1
Stanley Pl	51 F1	Thistle St S E La	42 C1
Stanley Rd	46 B2	Thistle St S W La	42 C1
Stanwell St	47 E4	Thomson's Ct **35**	42 C3
Starbank Rd	46 B2	Thorntree St	47 F4
Stead's Pl	47 E4	Thorntreeside	47 F4
Stenhouse Av	48 B5	Thornville Ter	47 F5
Stenhouse Av W	48 B6	Thornybauk	42 B3
Stenhouse Cres	48 B6	Timber Bush	47 F2
Stenhouse Cross	48 B6	Tinto Pl	46 D4
Stenhouse Dr	48 B6	Tipperlinn Rd	49 H6
Stenhouse Gdns	48 B6	Tolbooth Wynd	47 E3
Stenhouse Gdns N	48 B6	Torphichen Pl	42 A3
Stenhouse Gro	48 B6	Torphichen St	42 A3
Stenhouse Pl E	48 B6	Tower Pl	47 F2
Stenhouse Pl W	48 B6	Tower St	47 F2
Stenhouse St E	48 B6	Tower St La	47 F2
Stenhouse St W	48 A6	Townswomen's Guild Wk	43 D4
Stenhouse Ter	48 C6	Trafalgar La	46 C3
Stevenlaw's Cl	43 D2	Trafalgar St	46 C3
Stevenson Av	48 D5	Traquair Pk E	48 A4
Stevenson Dr	48 B6	Trinity Ct	46 A3
Stevenson Gro	48 D5	Trinity Cres	46 A1
Stevenson Rd	48 D5	Trinity Gro	46 A2
Stevenson Ter	48 D5	Trinity Mains	46 A3
Stewart Ter	49 E5	Trinity Rd	46 A2
Stewartfield	46 C4	Trinity Way	46 A3
Stirling Rd	46 A2	Tron Sq **46**	43 D2
Strachan Gdns	44 B6	Tynecastle La	49 F5
Strachan Rd	48 C1	Tynecastle Ter	49 F5
Stratheam Pl	50 A6	Tytler Gdns	43 F1
Stratheam Rd	50 B6		
Succoth Av	49 E2		
Succoth Ct	49 E2	**U**	
Succoth Gdns	49 E2	Ulster Cres	51 H2
Succoth Pk	48 D2	Ulster Dr	51 H2
Succoth Pl	49 E2	Union Pl **8**	43 E1
Summer Pl	46 B5	Union St	46 C6
Summerbank	46 B6	Upper Bow **26**	43 D2
Summerfield Gdns	47 G4	Upper Coltbridge Ter	49 E2
Summerfield Pl	47 G4	Upper Damside	49 G2
Summerhall **13**	50 D5	Upper Dean Ter	42 A1
Summerhall Cres **12**	43 E4	Upper Gilmore Pl	42 B4
Summerhall Pl **11**	50 D5	Upper Gilmore Ter	42 B4
Summerhall Sq	50 D5	Upper Gray St	50 D5
Summerside Pl	46 C3	Upper Greenside La **13**	43 E1
Summerside St	46 C3	Upper Gro Pl	42 A4
Sunbury Ms	49 G2	Upper Hermitage	47 F4
Sunbury Pl	49 G2		
Sunbury St	49 G2		
Sunnybank	51 G1	**V**	
Sunnybank Pl	51 G1	Valleyfield St	42 B4
Sunnybank Ter **11**	51 F1	Vanburgh Pl	47 F4
Sunnyside	47 F6	Veitch's Sq	46 A6
Surrey Pl **8**	49 F3	Vennel	42 C3
Sutherland St	49 F3	Ventnor Pl	51 F6
Swanfield	47 E3	Ventnor Ter	51 E6
Sylvan Pl	50 C5	Victoria Dock	47 E2
		Victoria St	43 D3
		Victoria Ter **37**	42 C3
T		Viewcraig Gdns	43 E2
Tanfield	46 B5	Viewcraig St	43 E2
Tantallon Pl	50 D5	Viewforth	42 A4
Tarvit St	42 B4	Viewforth Gdns	50 A5
Tay St	49 G5	Viewforth Sq	49 H5
Taylor Gdns	47 E3	Viewforth Ter	49 H5
Taylor Pl	51 F1	Violet Ter	49 F5
Telfer Subway	49 G4	Vivian Ter	44 A5
Telford Dr	45 E5		
Telford Gdns	45 E5		
Telford Pl	45 E5	**W**	
Telford Rd	45 E6	Walker St	42 A2
Temple Pk Cres	49 G5	Walker Ter **17**	42 A3
Tennant St	47 E4	Warden's Cl	43 D3
Terrars Cft	43 F4	Wardie Av	45 H3
Teviot Pl	43 D3	Wardie Cres	45 G2
Teviotdale Pl	46 A6	Wardie Dell	45 H2
Thirlestane La	50 B6		

Wardie Gro	45 G2	West Pk Pl	49 G4
Wardie Ho La	45 H1	West Pier	45 F1
Wardie Pk	45 H3	West Pilton Av	44 D4
Wardie Rd	45 H3	West Pilton Bk	44 C3
Wardie Sq	45 H2	West Pilton Cres	44 C3
Wardie Steps	45 H2	West Pilton Crossway	44 D3
Wardieburn Dr	45 G2	West Pilton Dr	44 D3
Wardieburn Pl E	45 G2	West Pilton Gdns	44 D3
Wardieburn Pl N	45 G2	West Pilton Grn	44 D3
Wardieburn Pl S	45 G2	West Pilton Gro	44 D4
Wardieburn Pl W	45 F2	West Pilton Lea	44 D3
Wardieburn Rd	45 F2	West Pilton Loan	44 D3
Wardieburn St E	45 F2	West Pilton March	45 E2
Wardieburn St W	45 F2	West Pilton Pk	44 D3
Wardieburn Ter	45 F2	West Pilton Pl	45 E3
Wardiefield	45 G2	West Pilton Ri	44 D3
Wardlaw Pl	49 F5	West Pilton Rd	45 E3
Wardlaw St	49 F5	West Pilton St	44 D3
Wardlaw Ter	49 F5	West Pilton Ter	44 D3
Warrender Pk Cres	50 A5	West Pilton Vw	44 D3
Warrender Pk Rd	50 B5	West Port	42 C3
Warrender Pk Ter	50 B5	West Preston St	50 D5
Warriston Av	46 B4	West Register St	43 D1
Warriston Cres	46 B5	West Register St La	43 D1
Warriston Dr	46 A4	West Richmond St	43 E3
Warriston Gdns	46 A4	West Scotland St La	46 B6
Warriston Gro	46 A4	West Shore Rd	44 C2
Warriston Pl	46 B5	West Shore Rd Trd Est	44 D1
Warriston Rd	46 B3	West Silvermills La	46 A6
Warriston Ter	46 A4	West Stanhope Pl **7**	49 F3
Washington La	49 G4	West Tollcross	42 B4
Washington St	49 G4	West Werberside	45 F4
Water St	47 F3	West Winnelstrae	45 G4
Waterloo Pl	43 D1	West Wds	45 F5
Water's Cl **6**	42 B1	Wester Cl **5**	46 C1
Watson Cres	49 G5	Wester Coates Av	49 F3
Waverley Br	43 D2	Wester Coates Gdns	49 F3
Waverley Pk	51 F1	Wester Coates Pl	49 F2
Waverley Pk Ter	51 F1	Wester Coates Rd	49 F3
Waverley Pl	51 F1	Wester Coates Ter	49 F3
Waverley St	43 D2	Wester Drylaw Av	44 C5
Websters Land **39**	42 C3	Wester Drylaw Dr	44 C5
Well Ct **23**	42 A2	Wester Drylaw Pk	44 D5
Wellington Pl	47 F3	Wester Drylaw Pl	44 C5
Wellington St	47 E6	Wester Drylaw Row	44 D6
Wemyss Pl	42 B1	Western Cor **1**	48 C3
Wemyss Pl Ms	42 B1	Western Gdns	48 D3
Werberside Ms	45 F4	Western Harbour	46 D1
West Adam St	43 E3	Western Pl	48 D3
West Annandale St	46 C5	Western Ter	48 D3
West App Rd	42 B3	Westfield Av	48 D5
West Bow	43 D3	Westfield Ct	48 D5
West Bowling Grn St	46 D3	Westfield Rd	49 E5
West Bryson Rd	49 G5	Westfield St	49 E5
West Castle Rd	49 H5	Westhall Gdns	50 A5
West Catherine Pl	49 F3	Wheatfield Pl	49 E5
West Cherrybank	46 B2	Wheatfield Rd	49 E5
West Coates	49 F3	Wheatfield St	49 E5
West College St	43 D3	Wheatfield Ter **1**	49 E5
West Ct	48 D1	White Horse Cl	43 F2
West Cromwell St **18**	47 E2	White Pk	49 F5
West Crosscauseway	43 E4	Whitehall Ct	44 C6
West End	42 B2	Whitehouse Loan	50 A5
West End Pl	49 G4	Whitehouse Ter	50 B6
West Ferryfield	45 H2	Whitingford	46 C3
West Fountain Pl	49 G4	Whitson Cres	48 C5
West Gorgie Pk	48 D6	Whitson Gro	48 C5
West Gra Gdns	50 C6	Whitson Pl E	48 C5
West Granton Access	45 E2	Whitson Pl W	48 C5
West Granton Rd	45 F2	Whitson Rd	48 C5
West Harbour Rd	45 F1	Whitson Ter	48 C5
West Maitland St	42 A3	Whitson Wk	48 B5
West Mayfield	51 E6	Whitson Way	48 C5
West Mill La	42 A2	Whyte Pl	51 F1
West Montgomery Pl	46 D6	Wilfrid Ter **5**	51 H1
West Newington Pl	50 D5	William St	42 A2
West Nicolson St	43 E3	William St La N E	42 A2
West Norton Pl	43 F1		

West Pk Pl	49 G4	William St	42 A2
West Pier	45 F1	William St La N W	42 A2
West Pilton Av	44 D4	William St La S E	42 A2
		William St La S W	42 A3
		Willowbank Row	46 C2
		Willowbrae Av	51 H2
		Willowbrae Rd	51 H2
		Wilson's Ct **24**	43 E2
		Windmill La	43 E4
		Windmill Pl **12**	43 E4
		Windmill St	43 D4
		Windsor St	46 D6
		Windsor St La	46 D6
		Wishaw Ter	51 G1
		Wolseley Cres	51 H1
		Wolseley Gdns **8**	51 H1
		Wolseley Pl **9**	51 H1
		Wolseley Ter **6**	51 H1
		Woodbine Ter	47 F5
		Woodville Ter	47 F5
		Wright's Hos	50 A5
		Wyvern Pk	50 C6
		Y	
		Yardheads	47 E3
		Yeaman La	49 G4
		Yeaman Pl	49 G4
		York La	43 D1
		York Pl	43 D1
		York Rd	46 B2
		Young St	42 B2
		Young St La N	42 B2
		Young St La S	42 B2
		Z	
		Zetland Pl	46 A2

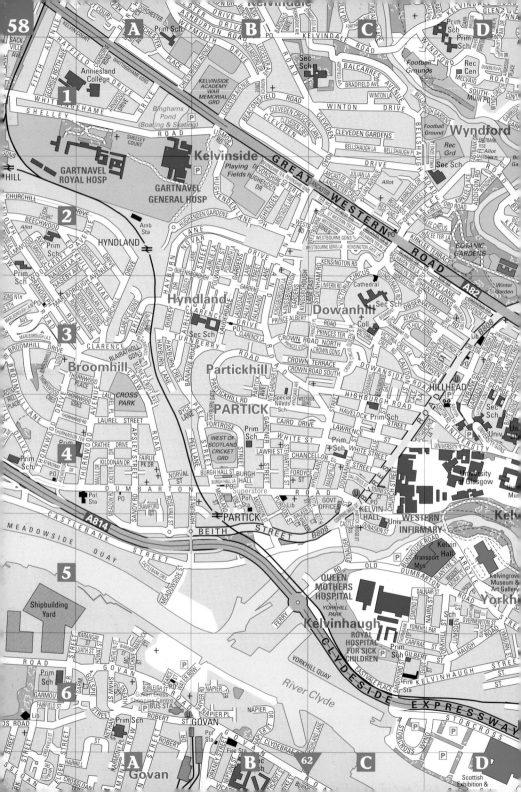

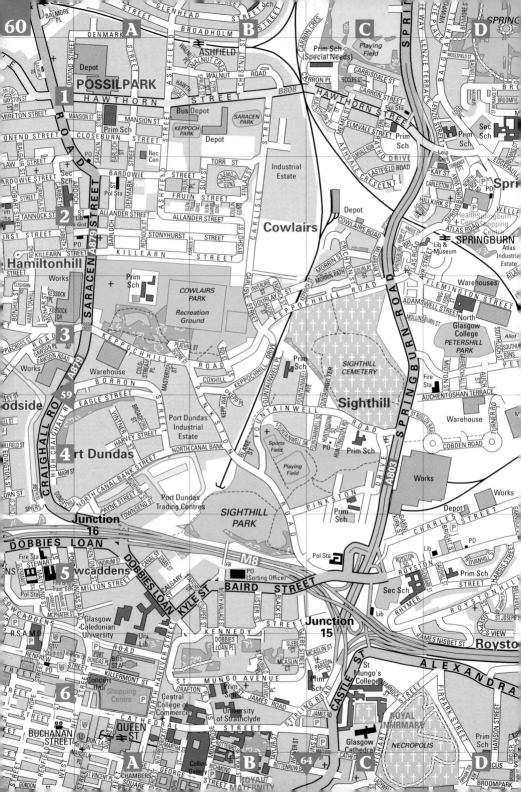

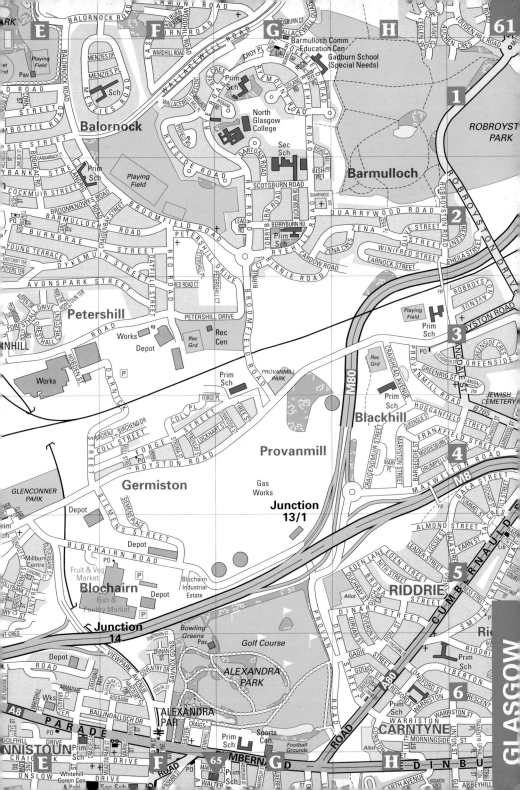

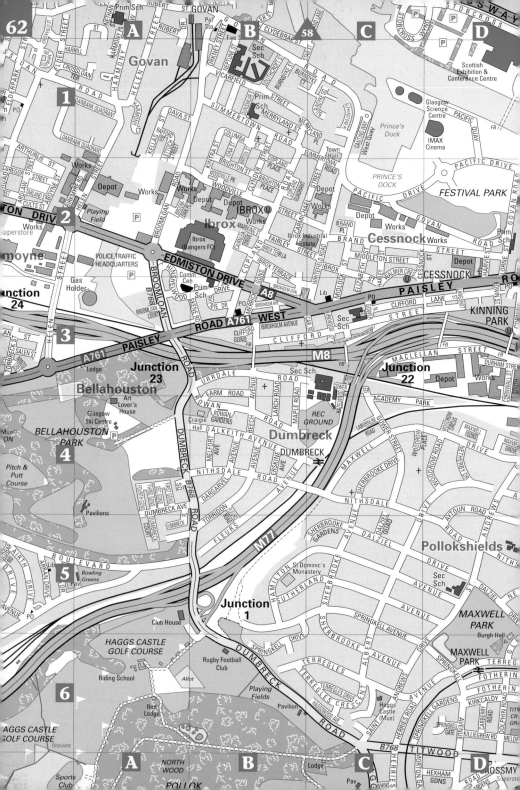

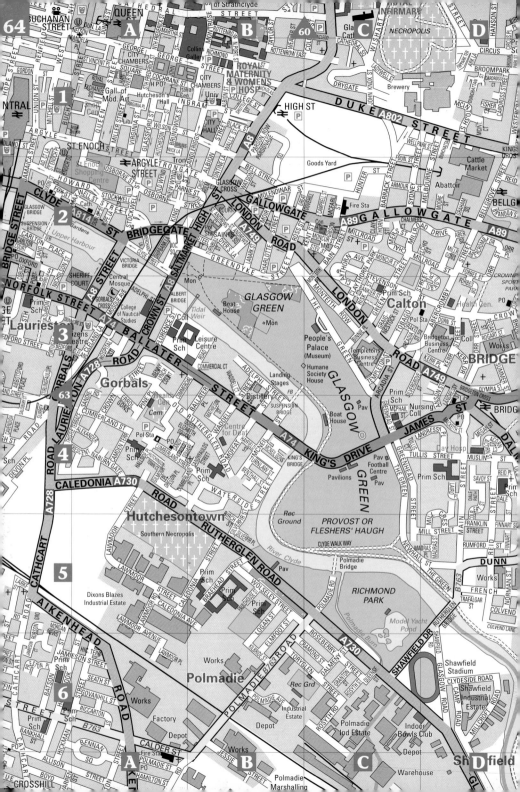

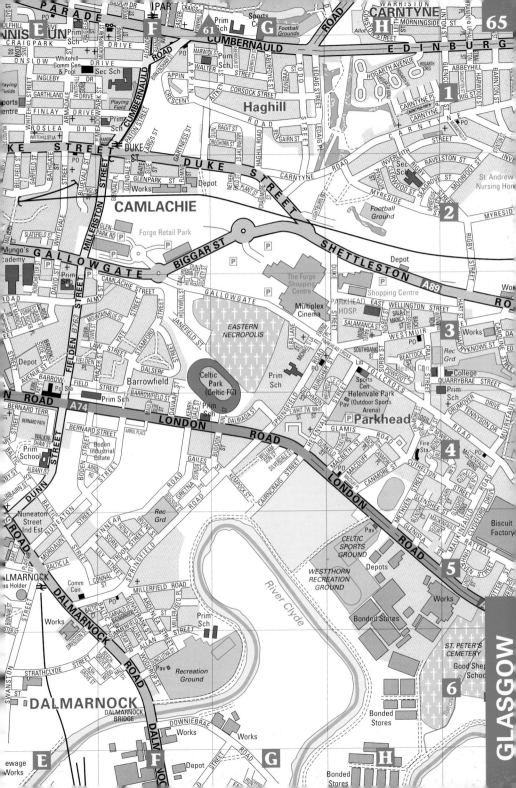

A

Abbotsford Place 63 H3
Abercromby Drive 64 D2
Abercromby 64 D2
Square
Abercromby Street 64 D3
Aberdour Street 65 G1
Aberfeldy Street 65 G1
Aberfoyle Street 65 G1
Abernethy Street 65 G1
Academy Park 62 C4
Acorn Court 64 D4
Acorn Street 64 D4
Adams Court Lane 63 H2
Adamswell Street 60 C3
Addison Road 58 D2
Adelphi Street 64 B3
Admiral Street 63 E3
Aikenhead Road 63 H5
Aird's Lane 64 A2
  Bridgegate
Airlie Lane 58 B2
Airlie Street 58 A3
Aitken Street 65 G1
Albany Street 65 E4
Albert Bridge 64 A3
Albert Cross 63 F5
Albert Drive 62 C6
Albion Gate 64 B1
  Albion Street
Albion Street 64 B2
Alexander Crescent 64 A4
Alexandra Court 61 F6
Alexandra Cross 65 F1
Alexandra Parade 60 D6
Alexandra Park 65 F1
Street
Alford Street 60 B3
Alfred Lane 58 D3
Allan Place 65 F5
Allan Street 65 F6
Allander Street 60 A2
Allison Place 63 G6
  Prince Edward Street
Allison Street 63 G6
Alma Street 65 E3
Almond Street 61 H5
Alston Lane 64 C2
  Claythorn Street
Amisfield Street 59 E1
Anchor Lane 64 A1
  Saint Vincent Place
Ancroft Street 59 G3
Anderson Street 58 B4
Anderston Cross 63 G1
Centre
Anderston Quay 63 F2
Angus Street 60 C2
Annandale Street 63 H5
Annbank Place 64 D2
Annbank Street 64 D2
Annette Street 63 G6
Annfield Place 64 D1
Anson Street 64 D4
Anthony Street 63 G1
Appin Crescent 65 F1
Appin Road 65 F1
Appleby Street 59 H3
Applecross Street 59 H3
Apsley Lane 58 A4
  Apsley Street
Apsley Street 58 A4
Arcadia Street 64 C3
Ardbeg Lane 63 G6
Ardbeg Street 63 G6
Ardenlea Street 65 F5
Ardery Street 58 A4
  Apsley Street
Ardessie Place 58 D1
Ardo Gardens 62 A3
  Hinshelwood Drive
Ardoch Street 60 A2
Argyle Street 63 G1
Argyll Arcade 64 A1
Ark Lane 64 D1

Arlington Street 59 F5
Armadale Court 61 E6
Armadale Path 61 E6
Armadale Place 61 E6
Armadale Street 65 E1
Armour Street 64 C2
Arnwood Drive 58 A1
Arrol Place 65 F4
Arrol Road 65 E4
Arthur Street 58 D5
Ascog Street 63 G6
Ashfield Street 60 A2
Ashgrove Street 65 E6
Ashley Lane 59 F5
Ashley Street 59 F5
Ashton Lane 58 D4
Ashton Lane North 58 D4
  Ashton Lane
Ashton Road 58 D4
Ashvale Crescent 60 C1
Aspen Drive 61 E3
Athole Gardens 58 C3
Athole Lane 58 C3
Atlas Industrial 60 D2
Estate
Atlas Place 60 D2
Atlas Road 60 C2
Atlas Square 60 D2
  Ayr Street
Auchentoshan 60 D4
Terrace
Auchinloch Street 60 D3
Auckland Street 59 H3
Avenue Street 65 E3
Avenuepark Street 59 E2
Avonspark Street 61 E3
Ayr Street 60 C2
Aytoun Road 62 D5

B

Back Causeway 65 H3
Bagnell Street 60 D1
Bain Square 64 C2
  Bain Street
Bain Street 64 C2
Baird Street 60 B5
Bairds Brae 59 H3
Balaclava Street 63 G1
  McAlpine Street
Balcarres Avenue 58 C1
Balgair Street 59 H1
Balglass Street 59 H2
Balgraybank Street 60 D2
Balgrayhill Road 60 D1
Baliol Lane 59 F5
Baliol Street 59 F5
Ballater Place 64 B4
Ballater Street 64 A3
Ballindalloch Drive 61 E6
Ballindarroch Lane 61 E6
  Armadale Street
Balmore Square 59 H1
Balornock Road 61 E1
Baltic Court 65 E5
  Baltic Street
Baltic Lane 65 E5
Baltic Place 65 E4
Baltic Street 65 E4
Banavie Lane 58 B3
  Banavie Road
Banavie Road 58 A3
Bank Street 59 E4
Bankhall Street 63 H6
Bankier Street 64 C3
Bannatyne 65 F1
Avenue
Barbreck Road 63 G6
  Pollokshaws Road
Barclay Street 60 D1
  Lenzie Street
Bardowie Street 59 H2
Bargeddie Street 61 H4
Barloch Street 60 A2
Barmulloch Road 61 E2

Barnhill Drive 61 E3
  Foresthall Drive
Barr Street 59 G3
Barrack Street 64 C2
Barrington Drive 59 F4
Barrland Street 63 G5
Barrowfield Street 65 E3
Bartholomew 65 E5
Street
Bath Lane 59 G6
  Wellington Street
Bath Lane West 59 F6
  North Street
Bath Street 59 G6
Bathgate Street 65 E2
Batson Street 63 H6
Beaconsfield Road 58 B1
Beaton Road 63 E6
Beattock Street 65 H3
Beaumont Gate 58 C3
Bedford Lane 63 H3
Bedford Street 63 H3
Beech Avenue 62 B3
Beechgrove Street 65 F6
Beith Street 58 B5
Belgrave Lane 59 E3
Belgrave Terrace 59 E3
Belhaven Crescent 58 C2
Lane
  Kensington Road
Belhaven Terrace 58 C2
Belhaven Terrace 58 C2
Lane
Belhaven Terrace 58 C2
West
  Blythswood Street
Belhaven Terrace 58 C2
West Lane
Bell Street 64 B2
Bellevue Place 60 D5
Bellfield Street 65 E2
Bellgrove Street 64 D2
Bellshaugh 58 C1
Gardens
Bellshaugh Lane 58 C1
Bellshaugh Place 58 C1
Bellshaugh Road 58 C1
Belmont Crescent 59 E3
Belmont Lane 59 E3
Belmont Street 59 E3
Beltane Street 59 F6
  Dorset Street
Benalder Street 58 C5
Bengairn Street 65 G1
Bennan Square 64 A6
Benny Lynch 64 A3
Court
Benthall Street 64 B4
Bentinck Street 59 E5
Benview Street 59 F2
Berkeley Street 59 E6
Berkeley Terrace 59 F6
Lane
  Elderslie Street
Bernard Path 65 E4
Bernard Street 65 E4
Bernard Terrace 65 E4
Berryburn Road 61 G2
Biggar Street 65 F2
Bilsland Court 59 H1
Bilsland Drive 59 F1
Binnie Place 64 C3
Birch Street 64 B5
  Silverfir Street
Birchend Drive 61 F4
Birchend Place 61 E4
Birkenshaw Street 65 F1
Birkwood Street 65 F6
  Dalmarnock Road
Birnam Road 65 H5
  London Road
Birnie Court 61 G3
Birnie Road 61 G2
Bishop Street 63 G1
Bishopmill Place 61 G2
Bishopmill Road 61 G1

Black Street 60 B5
Blackburn Street 62 D2
Blackfriars Street 64 B1
Blackie Street 58 D6
Blackthorn Street 60 C1
Blairatholl Avenue 58 A3
Blairatholl 58 A3
Gardens
Blane Street 60 B4
Blantyre Street 58 D5
Blochairn Road 61 E5
Bluevale Street 65 E2
Blythswood Court 63 G1
  Cadogan Street
Blythswood Square 59 G6
  Blythswood Street
Blythswood Street 63 G1
Boden Industrial 65 F4
Estate
Boden Street 65 E4
Boghead Road 61 E1
Bogside Street 65 F4
Boleyn Road 63 E6
Bonawe Street 59 F2
  Kirkland Street
Boness Street 65 F4
Bonhill Street 59 H3
Bonnar Street 65 E5
Borron Street 60 A3
Botanic Crescent 58 D2
Botanic Crescent 58 D2
Lane
Bothwell Lane 63 G1
  Blythswood Street
Bothwell Street 59 G6
Boundary Road 64 C6
  Rutherglen Road
Bower Street 59 E3
Bowman Street 63 G6
Bowmont Gardens 58 C3
Bowmont Terrace 58 C3
Bradfield Avenue 58 C1
Braehead Street 64 B5
Braemore Gardens 60 B2
Braeside Street 59 F3
Braid Square 59 G4
Braid Street 59 G4
Brand Place 62 C2
Brand Street 62 C2
Brandon Street 64 D2
Breadalbane Street 59 F6
  Saint Vincent Street
Brechin Street 59 E6
Bridge Street 63 H2
Bridgegate 64 A2
Bridgegate Path 64 A2
  Bridgegate
Bridgeton 64 D3
  Business Centre
Bridgeton Cross 64 D3
Bright Street 60 D5
Brighton Place 62 B2
Brighton Street 62 B2
Briton Street 62 B2
Broad Street 64 D3
Broadford Street 60 A4
Brodick Street 61 E5
Brook Street 64 D3
Brookside Street 65 E3
Broomfield Lane 60 D1
Broomfield Place 60 D1
Broomfield Road 60 D1
Broomielaw 63 G2
Broomknowes 61 E2
Road
Broomloan Court 62 A3
Broomloan Place 62 A2
Broomloan Road 62 A2
Broompark Circus 60 D6
Broompark Drive 64 D1
Broompark Lane 64 D1
Broompark Street 64 D1

Brown Street 63 G1
Bruce Road 63 E4
Brunswick Lane 64 A1
Brunswick Street 64 A1
Buccleuch Lane 59 G5
  Rose Street
Buccleuch Street 59 G5
Buchan Street 63 H3
  Norfolk Street
Buchanan Street 63 H1
Buckingham Street 58 D3
Buckingham 58 D3
Terrace
Bucksburn Road 61 G2
Buddon Street 65 G4
Bunhouse Road 58 C5
Burgh Hall Lane 58 B4
Burgh Hall Street 58 B4
Burgh Lane 58 D3
Burgher Street 65 G3
Burleigh Street 58 A6
Burmola Street 59 H2
Burnbank Gardens 59 F4
Burnbank Lane 59 F4
  Napiershall Street
Burnbank Place 64 C1
  Drygate
Burnbank Place 59 G4
(Woodside)
  Burnbank Terrace
Burnbank Terrace 59 F4
Burnbrae Street 61 E2
Burndyke Court 62 B1
Burndyke Square 62 C1
Burndyke Street 62 B1
Burns Street 59 H4
Burrells Lane 64 C1
Bute Gardens 58 D4
Bute Lane 58 D4
  Great George Street
Butterbiggins Road 63 G5
Butterfield Place 63 G5
  Pollokshaws Road
Byres Road 58 C4
Byshot Street 60 B2

C

Cadogan Street 63 G1
Cadzow Street 63 G1
Caird Drive 58 B4
Cairncraig Street 65 G4
Cairnlea Drive 62 B2
Caithness Street 59 F2
Caldarvan Street 59 H3
Calder Street 63 H6
Caledon Lane 58 C3
Caledon Street 58 C3
Caledonia Avenue 64 A5
Caledonia Road 63 H4
Caledonia Street 64 A5
Caledonian 59 E4
Crescent
  Great Western Road
Calgary Street 60 A5
Callander Street 59 G3
Calton Entry 64 C2
  Gallowgate
Cambridge Street 59 H5
Camden Terrace 64 A4
Camlachie Street 65 F3
Camp Road 64 D6
Campsie Street 60 D1
Canal Street 60 A5
Candleriggs 64 B2
Canmore Place 65 H4
Canmore Street 65 H4
Canting Way 62 C1
Carberry Road 62 D6
Carbeth Street 59 H2
Carbisdale Street 60 C1
Carbrook Street 61 E5
Cardarrach Street 61 E1
Cardow Road 61 G2
Cardross Court 61 H5

Cardross Street 64 D1
Cardwell Street 63 G4
Eglinton Street
Cardyke Street 61 E2
Carfin Street 63 H6
Carfrae Street 58 C6
Carillon Road 62 C3
Carleston Street 60 D2
Carlisle Street 60 B2
Carlton Court 63 H1
Carlton Place 63 H2
Carmichael Street 62 B2
Carnarvon Street 59 F5
Carnoustie Place 63 F3
Carnoustie Street 63 F3
Carntyne Path 65 H1
Carntyne Place 65 H1
Carntyne Road 65 G2
Carrick Street 63 G2
Carrington Street 59 F4
Carron Crescent 60 B1
Carron Place 60 B1
Carron Street 60 C1
Carstairs Street 65 E6
Castle Crescent 64 A1
North Court
Royal Exchange Square
Castle Street 60 C6
Castle Street 58 C5
(Partick)
Castlebank 58 A5
Crescent
Cathedral Square 64 C1
Cathedral Street 60 A6
Catherine Place 63 F1
Hydepark Street
Cavendish Court 63 H4
Cavendish Place 63 H4
Cavendish Street 63 H4
Cecil Street 58 D3
Cedar Court 59 G4
Cedar Street 59 G4
Central Station 63 H1
Centre Street 63 G3
Cessnock Street 62 C2
Chalmers Court 64 C2
Chalmers Gate 64 C2
Claythorn Street
Chalmers Place 64 C2
Claythorn Street
Chalmers Street 64 C2
Chancellor Street 58 B4
Chapel Street 59 E1
Chapman Street 63 G6
Allison Street
Charing Cross 59 F6
Charing Cross Lane 59 F6
Granville Street
Charles Street 60 C5
Charlotte Lane 64 B2
London Road
Charlotte Lane 64 B2
South
Charlotte Street
Charlotte Lane 64 B2
West
London Road
Charlotte Street 64 B2
Cheapside Street 63 F2
Chelmsford Drive 58 B1
Chesterfield 58 A1
Avenue
Chestnut Street 60 B1
Chisholm Street 64 B2
Christopher Street 61 E4
Church Street 58 C4
Churchill Drive 58 A3
Circus Drive 64 D1
Circus Place 64 D1
Circus Place Lane 60 D6
Civic Street 59 H4
Clairmont Gardens 59 F5
Clare Street 61 E4
Claremont Passage 59 F5
Claremont Terrace

Claremont Place 59 F5
Claremont Terrace
Claremont Street 59 E6
Claremont Terrace 59 F5
Claremont Terrace 59 E5
Lane
Clarence Drive 58 A3
Clarence Gardens 58 A3
Clarence Lane 58 B3
Clarendon Lane 59 G4
Clarendon Street
Clarendon Place 59 G4
Clarendon Street 59 G4
Clayslaps Road 58 D5
Claythorn Avenue 64 C3
Claythorn Circus 64 C2
Claythorn Avenue
Claythorn Court 64 C2
Claythorn Park
Claythorn Park 64 C3
Claythorn Street 64 C2
Claythorn Terrace 64 C2
Claythorn Park
Clayton Terrace 64 D1
Cleghorn Street 59 H3
Cleland Lane 64 A3
Cleland Street 64 A3
Clerwood Street 65 H2
Cleveden Crescent 58 B1
Cleveden Crescent 58 B1
Lane
Cleveden Drive 58 B1
Cleveden Drive 58 C2
Lane
Mirrlees Drive
Cleveden Gardens 58 C1
Cleveland Lane 59 F6
Kent Road
Cleveland Street 59 F6
Cliff Road 59 F5
Clifford Gardens 62 B3
Clifford Lane 62 C3
Clifford Place 62 D2
Clifford Street
Clifford Street 62 B3
Clifton Place 59 E5
Clifton Street
Clifton Street 59 E5
Closeburn Street 60 A1
Clouston Court 59 E2
Fergus Drive
Clouston Lane 59 E2
Clouston Street 58 D2
Cloverbank Street 61 E5
Clutha Street 62 D2
Paisley Road West
Clyde Industrial 59 E6
Centre
Clyde Place 63 G2
Clyde Street 63 H2
Clydebrae Street 58 B6
Clydeside 58 C6
Expressway
Clydeside Road 64 D6
Clynder Street 62 B2
Coalhill Street 65 F3
Cobden Road 60 D4
Coburg Street 63 H3
Cochrane Street 64 A1
Cockmuir Street 61 E2
Colbert Street 64 D5
Coldstream Place 60 A3
Colebrooke Lane 59 E3
Colebrooke Street
Colebrooke Place 59 E3
Colebrooke Street 59 E3
Colebrooke 59 E3
Terrace
Coll Place 61 F4
Coll Street 61 F4
College Street 64 B1
Collins Street 64 C1
Columba Street 62 B1
Colvend Lane 64 D5
Colvend Street 64 D5

Comelypark Place 65 E2
Comelypark Street
Comelypark Street 64 D2
Commerce Street 63 H3
Commercial Court 64 B3
Commercial Road 64 A4
Congress Road 62 D1
Congress Way 63 E1
Connal Street 65 F5
Contin Place 58 D1
Cook Street 63 G3
Coopers Well Lane 58 C5
Dumbarton Road
Coopers Well Street 58 C5
Copland Place 62 B1
Copland Quadrant 62 B2
Copland Road 62 B2
Coplaw Street 63 G5
Corn Street 59 H4
Cornhill Street 61 E1
Cornwall Street 62 D3
Cornwall Street 62 D4
South
Corsock Street 65 G1
Corston Street 61 H6
Corunna Street 59 E6
Cotton Street 65 E6
Coulin Gardens 60 B2
Couper Street 60 B5
Coventry Drive 61 F6
Cowan Lane 59 E4
Cowan Street 59 E4
Cowcaddens Road 59 H5
Cowlairs Road 60 C2
Coxhill Street 60 B3
Craigenbay Street 61 F2
Craigendmuir 61 H4
Street
Craighall Road 59 H4
Craighead Avenue 61 H3
Craigie Street 63 G6
Craigiehall Place 62 D2
Craigiehall Street 62 D2
Craigiehall Place
Craigielea Street 61 E6
Craigmaddie 59 E5
Terrace Lane
Derby Street
Craigmont Drive 59 E1
Craigmore Street 65 G2
Craignethan 58 B4
Gardens
Lawrie Street
Craigpark 65 E1
Craigpark Drive 65 E1
Craigpark Terrace 65 E1
Craigpark
Crail Street 65 H3
Cramond Street 64 B6
Cranborne Road 58 A1
Cranston Street 59 F6
Cranworth Lane 58 D3
Cranworth Street 58 D3
Crathie Drive 58 A4
Crathie Lane 58 A4
Exeter Drive
Crawford Lane 58 A4
Crawford Street
Crawford Path 58 A4
Crawford Street
Crawford Street 58 A4
Cresswell Lane 58 D3
Cresswell Street 58 D3
Crichton Place 60 C2
Crichton Street
Crichton Street 60 C2
Crieff Court 59 F6
North Street
Crimea Street 63 G1
Crinan Street 61 F6
Croftbank Street 60 D2
Cromer Street 59 F1
Cromwell Lane 59 G4
Cromwell Street 59 G4
Crow Road 58 A3

Crown Circus 58 C3
Crown Court 64 A1
Virginia Street
Crown Gardens 58 C3
Crown Mansions 58 B3
North Gardner Street
Crown Road North 58 B3
Crown Road South 58 B3
Crown Street 64 A3
Crown Terrace 58 B3
Crownpoint Road 64 D3
Croy Place 61 G1
Croy Road 61 G1
Cubie Street 64 D3
Culloden Street 61 F6
Cumberland 64 A4
Arcade
Sandyfaulds Square
Cumberland Place 64 A4
Cumberland Street 63 H3
Cumbernauld Road 65 F1
Custom House 64 A2
Quay
Clyde Street
Cuthbertson Street 63 G6
Cuthelton Street 65 H4
Cuthelton Terrace 65 H4
Cypress Street 60 B1

D

Daisy Street 63 H6
Dalcross Lane 58 C4
Byres Road
Dalcross Street 58 C4
Dale Path 64 D4
Dale Street 64 D4
Dalhousie Lane 59 G5
Dalhousie Street
Dalhousie Street 59 G5
Dalintober Street 63 G3
Dalkeith Avenue 62 B4
Dalmally Street 59 F3
Dalmarnock Bridge 65 F6
Dalmarnock Court 65 F5
Dalmarnock Road 64 D4
Dalmeny Street 64 C6
Dalnair Street 58 C5
Dalriada Street 65 G4
Dalserf Street 65 F3
Dalziel Drive 62 C5
Dalziel Quadrant 62 C5
Dargarvel Avenue 62 B4
Dargarvel Path 62 A5
Dumbreck Avenue
Darnick Street 61 F3
Darnley Gardens 63 E6
Darnley Place 63 E6
Darnley Road
Darnley Road 63 E6
Darnley Street 63 F6
Dartford Street 59 H3
Dava Street 62 A1
Davaar Street 65 F4
David Street 65 E3
Davidson Street 65 E6
Dawson Place 59 H3
Dawson Road 59 H3
Deanside Lane 64 B1
Rottenrow
Dechmont Street 65 G3
Dee Street 61 H5
Denham Street 59 H3
Denmark Street 60 A2
Derby Street 59 E5
Derby Terrace Lane 59 E5
Derwent Street 59 H2
Deveron Street 61 H5
Devon Place 63 H4
Devon Street 63 H4
Devonshire 58 B2
Gardens
Devonshire 58 B2
Gardens Lane
Hyndland Road

Devonshire Terrace 58 B2
Devonshire Terrace 58 B2
Lane
Dick Street 59 F3
Dinart Street 61 H5
Dinwiddie Street 61 G4
Dixon Street 63 H2
Dixons Blazes 64 A5
Industrial Estate
Dobbies Loan 59 H5
Dobbies Loan Place 60 B6
Dolphin Road 62 D6
Don Street 61 H6
Doncaster Street 59 G2
Dora Street 64 D5
Dornoch Street 64 D3
Dorset Square 59 F6
Dorset Street
Dorset Street 59 F6
Douglas Lane 59 G6
West Regent Street
Douglas Street 59 G6
Douglas Terrace 63 F5
Glencairn Drive
Doune Gardens 59 E3
Doune Gardens 59 E3
Lane
Doune Quadrant 59 E3
Dover Street 59 E6
Dowanhill Street 58 C3
Dowanside Lane 58 D3
Byres Road
Dowanside Road 58 C3
Downiebrae Road 65 F6
Downs Street 60 D2
Drake Street 64 C3
Dreghorn Street 65 G1
Drem Place 58 B4
Merkland Street
Drumbottie Road 61 E1
Drumpellier Street 61 H4
Drury Street 63 H1
Renfield Street
Dryburgh Gardens 59 F3
Wilton Street
Drygate 64 C1
Duchray Lane 61 H5
Duchray Street 61 H5
Dudley Drive 58 A3
Dudley Lane 58 A3
Duke Street 64 C1
Dumbarton Road 58 A4
Dumbreck Avenue 62 A4
Dumbreck Court 62 A5
Dumbreck Path 62 A4
Dumbreck Avenue
Dumbreck Place 62 A5
Dumbreck Road 62 B5
Dumbreck Square 62 A4
Dunard Street 59 F2
Dunaskin Street 58 C5
Dunbeith Place 58 D1
Dunblane Street 59 H5
Dunchattan Place 64 D1
Dunchattan Street 64 D1
Dunclutha Street 65 F6
Dundas Lane 60 A6
Dundas Street 60 A6
Dundashill 59 H4
Dundasvale Court 59 H5
Maitland Street
Dundasvale Road 59 H5
Maitland Street
Dundonald Road 58 C2
Dunearn Street 59 F4
Dunkeld Street 65 G4
Dunlop Street 64 A2
Dunmore Lane 59 H3
Norfolk Street
Dunmore Street 64 A3
Dunn Street 65 E4
Dunolly Street 61 E5
Dunragit Street 65 G1
Dunrobin Street 65 F2
Dunsmuir Street 62 B1

Duntroon Street 61 F6
Durham Street 62 D3
Dyce Lane 58 A4
Dyer's Lane 64 B2
Dykemuir Place 61 F2
  Dykemuir Street
Dykemuir Quadrant 61 E2
  Dykemuir Street
Dykemuir Street 61 E2

E
Eagle Street 60 A4
Eaglesham Court 63 E2
  Blackburn Street
Eaglesham Place 63 E2
Earnock Street 61 H2
East Bath Lane 60 A6
  Sauchiehall Street
East Campbell 64 C2
Street
East Wellington 65 H3
Street
East Whitby Street 65 G4
Eastbank Drive 58 D1
Eastbank Place 58 D1
Eastbank Rise 58 D1
Eastburn Road 61 F1
Eastcroft Terrace 61 E2
Eastercraigs 61 F6
Eastfield Road 60 C2
Eastvale Place 58 C6
Eccles Street 60 C1
  Carron Street
Edelweiss Terrace 58 B4
  Gardner Street
Eden Lane 61 H5
Eden Street 61 H5
Edgefauld Avenue 60 D3
Edgefauld Drive 60 D2
Edgefauld Place 60 D1
Edgefauld Road 60 D2
Edgehill Lane 58 A2
Edinburgh Road 65 H1
Edington Street 59 H4
Edwin Street 62 D3
Eglinton Court 63 H3
Eglinton Street 63 H3
Elba Lane 65 G3
  Gallowgate
Elcho Street 64 D2
Elderslie Street 59 F5
Eldon Court 58 B4
  Caird Drive
Eldon Street 59 E4
Elgin Street 65 E3
  Rowchester Street
Elie Street 58 C4
Elizabeth Street 62 C3
Ellesmere Street 59 G2
Elliot Place 59 E6
  Finnieston Street
Elliot Street 63 E1
Elmbank Crescent 59 G6
Elmbank Lane 59 F6
  North Street
Elmbank Street 59 G6
Elmbank Street 59 G6
Lane
Elmfoot Street 64 B6
Elmvale Row 60 C1
Elmvale Row East 60 C1
  Elmvale Row
Elmvale Row West 60 C1
  Elmvale Row
Elmvale Street 60 C1
Elphinstone Place 62 C1
Eltham Street 59 H3
  Bonhill Street
Endrick Street 60 B3
Errol Gardens 64 A4
Erskine Avenue 62 B4
Esmond Street 58 C5
Eton Lane 59 E4
Ewing Place 65 G3

Exchange Place 64 A1
  Buchanan Street
Exeter Drive 58 A4
Exeter Lane 58 A4
  Exeter Drive

F
Fairbairn Path 65 E4
  Ruby Street
Fairbairn Street 65 E4
Fairley Street 62 B2
Fairlie Park Drive 58 A4
Falfield Street 63 G4
Falkland Lane 58 B3
Falkland Street 58 B3
Farm Road 62 B3
Farnell Street 59 H4
Fauldhouse Street 64 B5
Fergus Court 59 E2
  Fergus Drive
Fergus Drive 59 E2
Fergus Lane 59 F2
Fernbank Street 60 C1
Ferry Road 58 B5
Fielden Place 65 E3
Fielden Street 65 E3
Findhorn Street 61 H6
Finlas Street 60 B2
Finlay Drive 65 E1
Finnart Square 64 D5
Finnart Street 64 D5
Finnieston Quay 63 E1
Finnieston Square 59 E6
  Finnieston Street
Finnieston Street 63 E1
Firhill Road 59 G2
Firhill Street 59 G2
Firpark Place 60 D6
  Firpark Street
Firpark Street 60 D6
Firpark Terrace 64 D1
First Gardens 62 A4
Fisher Court 64 D1
Fitzroy Lane 59 E6
Fitzroy Place 59 E5
  Royal Terrace
Fleming Street 65 F2
Flemington Street 60 D3
Fleurs Avenue 62 B4
Fleurs Road 62 B4
Florence Street 64 A3
Forbes Drive 64 D3
Forbes Street 64 D2
Ford Road 58 D2
Fordneuk Street 65 E3
Fordyce Street 58 B4
Foremount Terrace 58 B3
Lane
Foresthall Crescent 61 E3
Foresthall Drive 61 E3
Forge Place 61 F4
Forge Retail Park 65 F2
Forge Shopping 65 G3
Centre, The
Forge Street 61 F4
Forrest Street 65 E3
Forrestfield Street 61 E5
Forth Street 63 F5
Fortrose Street 58 B4
Fotheringay Lane 62 D6
Fotheringay Road 62 D6
Foundry Street 60 D2
Fountain Street 64 C2
Fountainwell 60 B3
Avenue
Fountainwell Drive 60 B4
Fountainwell Place 60 B4
Fountainwell Road 60 B4
Fountainwell 60 C4
Square
Fountainwell 60 C4
Terrace
Fourth Gardens 62 A4
Fox Street 63 H2

Foyers Terrace 61 E2
Francis Street 63 G4
Frankfield Street 61 H4
Franklin Street 64 D5
Frazer Street 65 E3
French Street 64 D5
Fruin Place 60 A2
Fruin Street 60 A2

G
Gadie Street 61 H6
Gadshill Street 60 D5
Gailes Street 65 F4
Gallowgate 64 B2
Gardner Street 58 B4
Garfield Street 65 E2
Garmouth Court 58 A6
Garnet Court 59 G5
  New City Road
Garnet Street 59 G5
Garnethill Street 59 G5
Garnkirk Street 60 C5
Garnock Street 60 D4
Garrioch Crescent 58 D1
Garrioch Drive 58 D1
Garrioch Gate 59 E1
  Garrioch Road
Garrioch Quadrant 58 D1
Garrioch Road 58 D2
Garriochmill Road 59 E3
Garriochmill Way 59 F3
  South Woodside Road
Garscube Cross 59 H4
Garscube Road 59 G3
Gartferry Street 60 D2
Garth Street 64 A1
  Glassford Street
Garthland Drive 65 E1
Gartness Street 65 F1
Gartons Road 61 G1
Garturk Street 63 H6
Garvald Court 65 E6
  Baltic Street
Garvald Street 65 F5
Gateside Street 65 F2
Gear Terrace 65 F6
General Terminus 63 F2
Quay
George Square 64 A1
George Street 64 A1
Gibson Street 59 E4
(Hillhead)
Gibson Street 64 C2
(Calton)
Gilbert Street 58 C6
Gilmour Place 64 A4
Girvan Street 61 H5
Gladstone Street 59 G4
Glamis Road 65 H4
Glasgow Bridge 63 H2
Glasgow Cross 64 B2
Glasgow Green 64 B3
Glasgow Road 64 D6
Glasgow Street 59 E3
Glassford Street 64 A1
Glebe Court 60 B6
Glebe Street 60 B5
Glenapp Street 63 F5
Glenbarr Street 60 D5
Glencairn Drive 62 D6
Glencairn Gardens 63 E6
Glencairn Lane 63 F6
Glendale Place 65 F2
Glendale Street 65 F2
Glendarvel 60 B2
Gardens
Glenfarg Street 59 G4
Glenisla Street 65 H5
Glenmavis Street 59 H5
Glenpark Road 65 F2
Glenpark Street 65 F2
Glenshee Court 65 H5
Glenshee Street 65 H4
Glentrool Gardens 60 A2

Gloucester Street 63 G3
Golfhill Drive 61 E6
Golfhill Terrace 60 D6
  Firpark Street
Golspie Street 58 A6
Goosedubbs 64 A2
  Stockwell Street
Gorbals Cross 64 A3
Gorbals Lane 63 H2
  Oxford Street
Gorbals Street 63 H4
Gordon Lane 63 H1
  Mitchell Street
Gordon Street 63 H1
Gorstan Place 58 C1
  Wyndford Road
Gough Street 61 H6
Gourlay Path 60 B3
  Endrick Street
Gourlay Street 60 B3
Gourock Street 63 G4
  Eglinton Street
Govan Cross 58 A6
  Govan Road
Govan Cross 58 A6
  Shopping Centre
Govan Road 62 C2
Govanhill Street 63 H6
Gower Lane 62 D3
  North Gower Street
Gower Street 62 C4
Gower Terrace 62 C3
Grace Street 63 F1
Grafton Place 60 A6
Graham Square 64 D2
Graignestock Place 64 C3
  London Road
Graignestock Street 64 C3
Granby Lane 58 D3
Grant Street 59 F5
Granton Street 64 C6
Granville Street 59 F6
Gray Street 59 E5
Great Dovehill 64 B2
Great George 58 D3
Street
Great Kelvin Lane 59 E4
  Glasgow Street
Great Western 59 E3
Road
Great Western 58 C2
Terrace
Great Western 58 C2
Terrace Lane
Green, The 64 C3
Green Street 64 C3
Greendyke Street 64 B2
Greenhead Street 64 C4
Greenlodge Terrace 64 C4
  Greenhead Street
Greenrig Street 61 H3
Gretna Street 65 F4
Grier Path 65 H3
  Crail Street
Grierson Lane 61 H6
  Lomax Street
Grierson Street 61 H6
Grosvenor Crescent 58 D3
Grosvenor 58 D3
  Crescent Lane
  Byres Road
Grosvenor Lane 58 D3
Grosvenor Terrace 58 D3
Grovepark Court 59 G4
Grovepark Gardens 59 G4
Grovepark Place 59 G3
Grovepark Street 59 G3
Gullane Street 58 B5
  Anderson Street

H
Haggswood 62 C6
Avenue
Haghill Road 65 G2

Haig Street 61 E2
Hallside Place 64 A4
Hamilton Avenue 62 D5
Hamilton Drive 59 E3
Hamilton Park 59 E3
Avenue
Hamiltonhill 59 H2
Crescent
  Hamiltonhill Road
Hamiltonhill Road 59 H3
Hanover Street 64 A1
Hanson Street 60 D6
Harcourt Drive 61 F6
Harley Street 62 C3
Harmony Court 62 A1
Harmony Place 62 A1
Harmony Row 62 A1
Harmony Square 62 A1
  Harmony Row
Harrison Drive 62 B2
  Copland Road
Harvey Street 60 A4
Harvie Street 62 D2
Hastie Street 58 D5
Hathaway Lane 59 E1
Hathaway Street 59 E1
Haugh Road 58 D6
Havelock Lane 58 C4
Havelock Street 58 C4
Hawthorn 60 A1
Quadrant
Hawthorn Street 60 A1
Hayburn Court 58 B4
  Hayburn Street
Hayburn Crescent 58 A3
Hayburn Gate 58 B4
Hayburn Lane 58 A3
Hayburn Street 58 B5
Hayfield Street 64 B4
Hayston Crescent 59 H1
Hayston Street 59 H1
Hazelwood Road 62 C4
Heddle Place 63 G1
  Cadogan Street
Helen Street 62 A1
Helenvale Court 65 H4
Helenvale Street 65 G4
Henderson Street 59 F3
Herbert Street 59 F3
Heron Street 64 D4
Herries Road 62 C6
Herriet Street 63 F5
Hickman Street 64 A6
Hickman Terrace 64 A6
Hickory Street 60 C1
High Craighall 59 H4
Road
High Street 64 B2
Highburgh Road 58 C3
Highland Lane 58 C6
Hill Street 59 G5
Hillfoot Street 65 E1
Hillhead Place 59 E4
  Bank Street
Hillhead Street 58 D4
Hillhouse Street 61 E2
Hillkirk Place 60 C2
  Hillkirk Street
Hillkirk Street 60 D2
Hillkirk Street Lane 60 D2
  Hillkirk Street
Hillsborough 59 E3
Terrace
  Bower Street
Hillside Gardens 58 B3
Lane
  North Gardner Street
Hinshaw Street 59 G3
Hinshelwood Drive 62 A2
Hobart Street 59 H2
Hobden Street 61 E3
Hogarth Avenue 65 H1
Hogarth Crescent 65 H1
Hogarth Drive 65 H1
Hogarth Gardens 65 H1

Hogganfield Street	61 H4	
Holland Street	59 G6	
Holly Drive	61 E3	
Hollybank Street	61 E5	
Hollybrook Place	64 A6	
Hollybrook Street		
Hollybrook Street	64 A6	
Holm Street	63 G1	
Holyrood Crescent	59 F4	
Holyrood Quadrant	59 F4	
Holywell Street	65 F3	
Hope Street	63 H1	
Hopefield Avenue	58 C1	
Hopehill Gardens	59 G3	
Hopehill Road	59 G3	
Hopetoun Terrace	61 E3	
Horne Street	60 C1	
Hawthorn Street		
Hornshill Street	61 E2	
Horselethill Road	58 C2	
Hospital Street	64 A3	
Hotspur Street	59 E1	
Houldsworth Lane	59 E6	
Houldsworth Street	59 E6	
Houston Place	63 F2	
Houston Street	63 F3	
Howard Street	63 H2	
Howat Street	58 A6	
Hughenden Drive	58 B2	
Hughenden Gardens	58 A2	
Hughenden Lane	58 B2	
Hughenden Road	58 B2	
Hughenden Terrace	58 B2	
Hughenden Road		
Hugo Street	59 F1	
Hunter Street	64 C2	
Huntingdon Road	60 C4	
Huntingdon Square	60 C4	
Huntly Gardens	58 C3	
Huntly Road	58 C3	
Hutcheson Street	64 A1	
Hutchinsontown Court	64 A4	
Hydepark Street	63 F1	
Hyndland Avenue	58 B4	
Hyndland Road	58 B2	
Hyndland Street	58 C4	

I

Ibrox Industrial Estate	62 C2	
Ibrox Street	62 C2	
Ibrox Terrace	62 B2	
Ibrox Terrace Lane	62 B2	
Ibroxholm Avenue	62 B3	
Ibroxholm Oval	62 B3	
Ibroxholm Place	62 B3	
Paisley Road West		
India Street	59 G6	
Ingleby Drive	65 E1	
Inglefield Street	63 H5	
Inglis Street	65 E2	
Ingram Street	64 A1	
Inverleith Street	65 H2	
Invershin Drive	58 D1	
Inverurie Street	60 B3	
Iona Street	62 B1	
Irongray Street	65 G1	
Irvine Street	65 F5	

J

Jamaica Street	63 H1	
James Morrison Street	64 B2	
Saint Andrews Square		
James Nisbet Street	60 C6	
James Street	64 C4	
James Watt Lane	63 G1	
James Watt Street		
James Watt Street	63 G1	
Jamieson Court	63 H6	

Jamieson Path	63 H6	
Jamieson Street		
Jamieson Street	63 H6	
Janefield Street	65 F3	
Jardine Street	59 F3	
Raeberry Street		
Jedburgh Gardens	59 F3	
Wilton Street		
Jessie Street	64 B6	
Jocelyn Square	64 A2	
John Knox Lane	64 C1	
Drygate		
John Knox Street	64 C1	
John Street	64 A1	
Julian Avenue	58 C2	
Julian Lane	58 C2	

K

Karol Path	59 G4	
Saint Peters Street		
Kay Street	60 D2	
Keir Street	63 F5	
Keith Court	58 C5	
Keith Street	58 C4	
Kelbourne Street	59 E2	
Kellas Street	62 A1	
Kelty Place	63 H3	
Bedford Street		
Kelvin Drive	58 D2	
Kelvin Way	58 D5	
Kelvingrove Street	59 E6	
Kelvinhaugh Place	58 D6	
Kelvinhaugh Street		
Kelvinhaugh Street	58 D6	
Kelvinside Avenue	59 F2	
Kelvinside Drive	59 F2	
Kelvinside Gardens	59 E2	
Kelvinside Gardens East	59 F3	
Kelvinside Gardens Lane	59 E2	
Kelvinside Terrace South	59 E3	
Kelvinside Terrace West	59 E3	
Kemp Street	60 C2	
Kempock Street	65 G4	
Kenmure Street	63 F6	
Kennedy Path	60 B6	
Saint Mungo Place		
Kennedy Street	60 B5	
Kennet Street	61 E5	
Kennyhill Square	61 F6	
Kensington Gate	58 C2	
Kensington Road		
Kensington Gate Lane	58 C2	
Kensington Road	58 C2	
Kent Road	59 E6	
Kent Street	64 C2	
Keppoch Street	60 B3	
Keppochhill Drive	60 B3	
Keppochhill Place	60 B4	
Keppochhill Road	60 B3	
Keppochhill Way	60 B4	
Kerr Drive	64 D3	
Kerr Place	64 D3	
Kerr Street	64 D3	
Kerrydale Street	65 F4	
Kersland Lane	58 D3	
Kersland Street	58 D3	
Kessock Drive	59 H3	
Kessock Place	59 H3	
Kew Gardens	58 D3	
Ruthven Street		
Kew Lane	58 D3	
Kew Terrace	58 D3	
Kilbarchan Street	63 H3	
Bedford Street		
Kilberry Street	61 E5	
Kilbirnie Place	63 G4	
Kilbirnie Street	63 G4	
Kilbride Street	64 B6	
Kildonan Drive	58 A4	

Kildrostan Street	63 F6	
Killearn Street	59 H2	
Killermont Street	60 A6	
Killiegrew Road	62 D6	
Kilmair Place	58 D1	
Kinbuck Street	60 B2	
King George Fifth Bridge	63 H2	
King Street	64 A2	
Kingarth Lane	63 G6	
Kingarth Street	63 G6	
King's Bridge	64 B4	
Kings Cross	64 D1	
King's Drive	64 C4	
Kingsborough Gardens	58 B3	
Kingsborough Gate	58 B3	
Prince Albert Road		
Kingsborough Lane	58 B3	
Kingsborough Lane East	58 B3	
Kingston Bridge	63 G2	
Kingston Industrial Estate	63 F3	
Kingston Street	63 G2	
Kinloch Street	65 G4	
Kinnear Road	65 F5	
Kinning Park Industrial Estate	63 F3	
Kinning Street	63 G3	
Kinnoul Lane	58 C3	
Dowanside Road		
Kintra Street	62 B1	
Kintyre Street	61 E5	
Kirkcaldy Road	62 D6	
Kirkhill Drive	59 E1	
Kirkhill Place	58 D1	
Kirkhill Drive		
Kirkland Street	59 F3	
Kirklee Circus	58 C2	
Kirklee Gardens	58 C1	
Kirklee Gardens Lane	58 D2	
Kirklee Place	58 D2	
Kirklee Quadrant	58 D2	
Kirklee Quadrant Lane	58 D2	
Kirklee Quadrant		
Kirklee Road	58 C2	
Kirklee Terrace	58 C2	
Kirklee Terrace Lane	58 C2	
Kirkmichael Avenue	58 A3	
Blairatholl Avenue		
Kirkmichael Gardens	58 A3	
Blairatholl Avenue		
Kirkpatrick Street	65 E3	
Kirkwood Street	62 C3	
Knowehead Gardens	63 E5	
Knowehead Terrace		
Knowehead Terrace	63 E5	
Kyle Street	60 A5	

L

La Belle Allee	59 E5	
La Belle Place	59 E5	
La Crosse Terrace	59 E3	
Laburnum Road	62 C4	
Ladywell Street	64 C1	
Laidlaw Street	63 G3	
Laird Place	64 D4	
Lambhill Quadrant	63 E3	
Lambhill Street	62 D3	
Lanark Street	64 B2	
Lancaster Crescent	58 C2	
Lancaster Crescent Lane	58 C2	
Lancaster Terrace	58 C2	
Lancaster Terrace Lane	58 C2	
Westbourne Gardens West		

Lancefield Quay	63 E1	
Lancefield Street	63 F1	
Landressy Place	64 C4	
Landressy Street	64 D4	
Lane Gardens	58 B3	
North Gardner Street		
Langbank Street	63 H3	
Eglinton Street		
Langrig Road	61 E2	
Langshot Street	62 D3	
Lansdowne Crescent	59 F4	
Lansdowne Crescent Lane	59 F4	
Larbert Street	59 H5	
Larch Road	62 B3	
Largs Street	65 F1	
Latheron Drive	58 D1	
Latheron Place	58 D1	
Latherton Drive		
Laudedale Lane	58 B3	
Lauderdale Gardens	58 B3	
Laurel Place	58 A3	
Laurel Street	58 A4	
Laurieston Road	63 H4	
Laverockhall Street	60 D3	
Law Street	65 E3	
Lawmoor Avenue	64 A5	
Lawmoor Place	64 A6	
Lawmoor Road	64 A5	
Lawmoor Street	64 A5	
Lawrence Street	58 C4	
Lawrie Street	58 B4	
Leadburn Road	61 G2	
Leader Street	61 H5	
Ledaig Place	65 G1	
Ledaig Street	65 G1	
Leicester Avenue	58 B1	
Leith Street	61 H6	
Lendel Place	62 D3	
Paisley Road West		
Leny Street	59 F2	
Lenzie Street	60 D1	
Lenzie Terrace	60 D1	
Leslie Road	63 E5	
Leslie Street	63 F5	
Lettoch Street	62 A1	
Leven Street	63 F5	
Leyden Court	59 E1	
Leyden Gardens	59 E1	
Leyden Street	59 E1	
Liberton Street	61 H6	
Lightburn Road	65 G2	
Lily Street	65 F5	
Lilybank Gardens	58 D4	
Lilybank Gardens Lane	58 D4	
Lilybank Lane	58 D4	
Lilybank Gardens		
Lilybank Terrace	58 D4	
Great George Street		
Lincluden Path	63 F4	
McCulloch Street		
Linfern Road	58 C3	
Lismore Road	58 B1	
Lister Street	60 B5	
Little Dovehill	64 B2	
Gallowgate		
Little Street	63 F1	
McIntyre Street		
Lloyd Street	61 E6	
Loanbank Quadrant	62 A1	
Lochgreen Street	61 H3	
Lockhart Street	61 F4	
Logan Street	64 B5	
Lomax Street	61 H6	
Lomond Street	59 H1	
London Arcade	64 B2	
London Road		
London Lane	64 B2	
London Road		
London Road	64 B2	
Longford Street	61 H6	
Lorne Street	62 D2	

Lorraine Gardens	58 C2	
Kensington Road		
Lorraine Gardens Lane	58 C2	
Westbourne Gardens Lane		
Lorraine Road	58 C2	
Kensington Road		
Lossie Street	61 H5	
Lothian Gardens	59 E3	
Wilton Street		
Loudon Terrace	58 D3	
Observatory Road		
Lovat Street	60 A4	
Borron Street		
Lowther Terrace	58 C2	
Redlands Lane		
Luath Street	58 A6	
Lumloch Street	61 E2	
Lumsden Street	58 D6	
Lymburn Street	58 D5	
Lyndhurst Gardens	59 F3	
Lyndhurst Gardens Lane	59 E2	
Lynedoch Crescent	59 F5	
Lynedoch Crescent Lane	59 F5	
Lynedoch Place	59 F5	
Lynedoch Street	59 F5	
Lynedoch Terrace	59 F5	

M

Macbeth Place	65 H4	
Macbeth Street	65 H4	
Macduff Place	65 H4	
Macduff Street	65 H4	
Mackeith Street	64 D4	
Mackie Street	60 A4	
Borron Street		
Mackinlay Street	63 H4	
Maclean Square	62 D2	
Maclean Street	62 D2	
Maclellan Street	62 C3	
Macleod Street	60 C6	
Madras Place	64 D5	
Madras Street	64 D5	
Mafeking Street	62 B2	
Main Street	64 D5	
Mair Street	63 E2	
Maitland Street	59 H5	
Malloch Street	59 E1	
Maltbarns Street	59 G3	
Malvern Court	65 E2	
Manresa Place	59 H4	
Mansel Street	60 D1	
Mansfield Street	58 C4	
Mansion Street	60 A1	
Maple Road	62 B4	
March Lane	63 F6	
Nithsdale Drive		
March Street	63 F6	
Marchmont Terrace	58 C3	
Observatory Road		
Marine Crescent	63 E2	
Marine Gardens	63 F2	
Mavisbank Gardens		
Mariscat Road	63 E6	
Marlow Street	63 E4	
Marne Street	65 F1	
Mart Street	64 A2	
Bridgegate		
Martha Street	60 A6	
Martin Street	64 D5	
Marwick Street	65 F1	
Mary Street	59 H4	
Maryhill Road	59 F3	
Maryhill Shopping Centre	59 E1	
Maryston Place	61 H4	
Maryston Street	61 H4	
Marywood Square	63 F6	
Masterton Street	60 A3	
Mathieson Street	64 B4	
Matilda Road	63 E5	

Mauchline Street 63 G4
Maukinfauld Court 65 H5
Mauldslie Street 63 F4
Maule Drive 58 A4
Mavisbank Gardens 63 E2
Maxwell Avenue 63 E4
Maxwell Court 63 E4
  Saint John's Road
Maxwell Drive 62 C4
Maxwell Gardens 62 D4
Maxwell Grove 62 D4
Maxwell Lane 63 E4
  Maxwell Drive
Maxwell Oval 63 F4
Maxwell Place 63 G5
Maxwell Road 63 F4
Maxwell Street 64 A2
Maxwell Terrace 63 E4
Maxwelton Road 61 H4
McAlpine Street 63 G1
McAslin Court 60 B6
McAslin Street 60 C6
McCulloch Street 63 F4
McFarlane Street 64 C2
McIntosh Court 64 D1
McIntosh Street 64 D1
McIntyre Street 63 F1
McKechnie Street 58 A6
McNeil Gardens 64 B4
McNeil Street 64 B4
McPhail Street 64 C4
McPhater Street 59 H5
Meadow Road 58 A4
Meadowpark 65 F1
  Street
Meadowside 58 A5
  Street
Megan Gate 64 D4
  Megan Street
Megan Street 64 D4
Melbourne Street 64 D2
Meldrum Gardens 62 D6
Melfort Avenue 62 B4
Melrose Gardens 59 F3
Melrose Street 59 F4
  Queens Crescent
Melvaig Place 58 D1
Melville Court 64 B2
  Brunswick Street
Melville Street 63 F5
Memel Street 60 C1
Menzies Drive 61 E1
Menzies Place 61 E1
Menzies Road 61 E1
Merchant Lane 64 A2
Merkland Court 58 B5
  Vine Street
Merkland Street 58 B4
Merrick Gardens 62 B3
Merrick Path 62 B3
  Merrick Gardens
Merryland Place 62 B1
Merryland Street 62 B1
Methven Street 65 H5
Metropole Lane 64 A2
  Clyde Street
Middlesex 63 E2
  Gardens
Middlesex Street 63 E3
Middleton Street 62 C2
Midland Street 63 H1
Midlock Street 62 C3
Midton Street 60 D3
Midwharf Street 60 A4
Migvie Place 58 D1
  Wyndford Road
Milan Street 63 G5
Mill Crescent 64 D5
Mill Street 64 D5
Millarbank Street 60 C2
Millburn Street 60 D5
Millcroft Road 64 D6
Miller Street 64 A1
Millerfield Place 65 F5
Millerfield Road 65 F5

Millerston Street 65 E2
Millroad Drive 64 C2
Millroad Gardens 64 D2
Millroad Street 64 C2
Milnbank Street 61 E6
Milnpark Gardens 62 D3
Milnpark Street 63 E3
Milton Street 60 A5
Minerva Street 59 E6
Minerva Way 59 E6
Mingarry Lane 59 E2
  Clouston Street
Mingarry Street 59 E2
Mireton Street 59 H1
Mirrlees Drive 58 C2
Mirrlees Lane 58 C2
Mitchell Lane 63 H1
Mitchell Street 63 H1
Moffat Street 64 B4
Moir Street 64 B2
Molendinar Street 64 B2
Mollinsburn Street 60 C3
Monar Drive 59 H3
  Monar Street
Monar Place 59 H3
  Monar Street
Monar Street 59 H3
Monart Place 59 F1
Moncur Street 64 C2
Monkscroft Avenue 58 A3
Monkscroft Court 58 A4
  Crow Road
Monkscroft 58 A3
  Gardens
  Monkscroft Avenue
Montague Lane 58 B2
Montague Street 59 F4
Monteith Place 64 C3
Monteith Row 64 C3
Monteith Row Lane 64 C3
  Monteith Place
Montgomery 65 E4
  Street
Montrose Street 60 B6
Moodiesburn 61 H4
  Street
Moore Street 64 D2
  Gallowgate
Moray Place 63 E6
Mordaunt Street 65 E5
Morgan Mews 63 H5
Morningside 61 H6
  Street
Morrin Path 60 C2
  Crichton Street
Morrin Square 60 C6
  Collins Street
Morrin Street 60 C2
Morrison Street 63 G2
Mosesfield Street 60 D1
Mosque Avenue 64 A3
Mount Street 59 F3
Mountainblue 65 E3
  Street
Moy Street 58 C4
  Church Street
Muirhead Street 58 B4
  Purdon Street
Muirpark Street 58 B4
  Gardner Street
Mull Street 61 F4
Murano Street 59 F2
Murdoch Street 60 D1
  Lenzie Street
Muslin Street 64 D4
Myreside Place 65 H2
Myreside Street 65 H2

N

Naburn Gate 64 A4
Nairn Street 58 D5
Nansen Street 59 G3
Napier Drive 58 B6
Napier Place 58 B6

Napier Road 58 B6
Napier Street 58 B6
Napier Terrace 58 B6
Napiershall Lane 59 F4
Napiershall Place 59 F4
  Napiershall Street
Napiershall Street 59 F4
Nelson Mandela 60 A6
  Place
Nelson Street 63 G2
Neptune Street 62 B1
Nethan Street 58 A6
Netherby Drive 62 D4
Netherfield Street 65 G2
New City Road 59 H5
New Wynd 64 A2
Newark Drive 62 D5
Newbank Gardens 65 H4
Newhall Street 64 C5
Newmill Road 61 G1
Newton Place 59 F5
Newton Street 59 G6
  Argyle Street
Newton Terrace 59 F6
  Sauchiehall Street
Newton Terrace 59 F6
  Lane
Nicholas Street 64 B1
Nicholson Lane 63 H2
  Nicholson Street
Nicholson Street 63 H2
Niddrie Road 63 F6
Niddrie Square 63 F6
Nisbet Street 65 H3
Nith Street 61 H5
Nithsdale Drive 63 F6
Nithsdale Place 63 F5
  Nithsdale Road
Nithsdale Road 63 F6
Nithsdale Street 63 F6
Norfolk Court 63 H3
Norfolk Lane 63 H3
  Norfolk Street
Norfolk Street 64 A3
Norman Street 64 D5
North Canal Bank 60 A4
North Canal Bank 60 A4
  Street
North Claremont 59 E5
  Street
  Royal Terrace
North Court 64 A1
  Saint Vincent Place
North Court Lane 64 A1
  Buchanan Street
North Frederick 64 A1
  Street
North Gardner 58 B4
  Street
North Gower 62 C3
  Street
North Hanover 60 A6
  Place
  North Hanover Street
North Hanover 60 A6
  Street
North Place 59 F6
  North Street
North Portland 64 B1
  Street
North Street 59 F6
North Wallace 60 B5
  Street
North Woodside 59 F3
  Road
Northcroft Road 60 D2
Northpark Street 59 F2
Northumberland 59 E2
  Street
Norval Street 58 A4
Norwich Drive 58 B1
Novar Drive 58 A2
Nuneaton Street 65 E5
Nuneaton Street 65 E5
  Industrial Estate

Nursery Lane 63 F6
Nursery Street 63 G5
  Pollokshaws Road

O

Oak Street 63 G1
Oakbank Industrial 59 H3
  Estate
Oakfield Avenue 59 E4
Oakfield Lane 59 E4
Oakley Terrace 64 D1
Oatfield Street 61 F2
Oban Court 59 E2
  Kelvinside Gardens
Oban Drive 59 E2
Oban Lane 59 E2
Observatory Lane 58 D3
  Observatory Road
Observatory Road 58 C3
Ogilvie Place 65 H4
Ogilvie Street 65 H4
Old Dalmarnock 64 D4
  Road
Old Dumbarton 58 C5
  Road
Old Rutherglen 64 A4
  Road
Old Wynd 64 A2
Olive Street 61 H2
Olympia Street 64 D3
Onslow Drive 65 E1
Onslow Square 65 E1
Oran Gardens 59 E1
Oran Gate 59 E1
Oran Place 59 E2
Oran Street 59 E1
Oregon Place 64 A4
Orkney Place 62 A1
  Orkney Street
Orkney Street 62 B1
Orr Place 64 D2
Orr Street 64 D2
Osborne Street 64 A2
Oswald Street 63 H1
Otago Lane 59 E4
Otago Lane North 59 E4
Otago Street 59 E4
Overnewton Place 58 D6
  Kelvinhaugh Street
Overnewton 58 D5
  Square
  Blackie Street
Overnewton Street 58 D5
Overtown Street 65 E3
Oxford Lane 63 H3
Oxford Street 63 H2

P

Pacific Drive 62 C2
Pacific Quay 62 D1
Paisley Road 63 G2
Paisley Road West 62 C3
Palermo Street 60 C2
  Atlas Road
Palmerston Place 58 D6
  Kelvinhaugh Street
Panmure Street 59 G2
Park Avenue 59 F4
Park Circus 59 E5
Park Circus Lane 59 E5
Park Circus Place 59 F5
Park Drive 59 E4
Park Gardens 59 E5
Park Gardens Lane 59 E5
Park Gate 59 E5
Park Quadrant 59 E5
Park Road 59 E4
Park Street South 59 E5
Park Terrace 59 E5
Park Terrace East 59 E5
  Lane
Park Terrace Lane 59 E5
Parkgrove Terrace 59 E5

Parkgrove Terrace 59 E5
  Lane
  Derby Street
Parkhead Cross 65 H3
Parnie Street 64 A2
Parson Street 60 C6
Parsonage Row 64 B1
Parsonage 64 B1
  Square
Partick Bridge 58 C4
  Street
Partickhill Avenue 58 B4
Partickhill Court 58 B3
Partickhill Road 58 B3
Paterson Street 63 G3
Patna Street 65 F5
Paton Street 65 F1
Payne Street 60 A4
Pearce Lane 58 A6
  Pearce Street
Pearce Street 58 A6
Peathill Street 60 A3
Peel Lane 58 B4
Peel Street 58 B4
Pembroke Street 59 F6
Penicuik Street 65 H2
Percy Street 62 D2
  Clifford Street
Perth Street 63 F1
  Argyle Street
Petershill Court 61 G2
Petershill Drive 61 F2
Petershill Place 61 F2
Petershill Road 60 D3
Phoenix Park 59 H4
  Terrace
  Corn Street
Phoenix Road 59 G5
  Great Western Road
Piccadilly Street 63 F1
Pine Place 64 A4
Pinkston Drive 60 C4
Pinkston Road 60 B3
Pitt Street 63 G1
Plant Street 65 G2
Plantation Park 62 D3
  Gardens
  Clifford Lane
Plantation Square 63 E2
Playfair Street 65 E5
Pointhouse Road 63 E1
Pollokshaws Road 63 G6
Pollokshields 63 F6
  Square
  Glencairn Drive
Polmadie Avenue 64 B6
Polmadie Industrial 64 C6
  Estate
Polmadie Road 64 C5
Polwarth Lane 58 B2
Polwarth Street 58 B3
Poplar Road 62 B3
  Urrdale Road
Poplin Street 64 D5
Port Dundas 60 A4
  Industrial Estate
Port Dundas Place 60 A6
Port Dundas Road 59 H5
Port Dundas 60 A4
  Trading Centres
Port Street 59 F6
Porter Street 62 C3
  Clifford Street
Portman Place 59 E4
  Cowan Street
Portman Street 63 E3
Portugal Lane 63 H3
  Bedford Street
Portugal Street 63 H3
Possil Cross 60 A3
Possil Road 59 H3
Powfoot Street 65 H3
Preston Place 63 H6
Preston Street 63 H6
Prince Albert Road 58 B3

Prince Edward 63 G6
  Street
Prince's Dock 62 C1
Princes Gardens 58 B3
Princes Place 58 C3
Princes Square 64 A1
  Buchanan Street
Princes Terrace 58 C3
Provan Road 61 G5
Provanhill Street 60 D5
Provanmill Place 61 H3
  Provanmill Road
Provanmill Road 61 H3
Purdon Street 58 B4

Q
Quarrywood 61 G2
  Avenue
Quarrywood Road 61 H2
Queen Elizabeth 64 B4
  Square
Queen Margaret 59 E2
  Court
  Fergus Drive
Queen Margaret 58 D3
  Drive
Queen Margaret 59 E2
  Road
Queen Mary Street 64 D4
Queen Square 63 F6
Queen Street 64 A1
Queens Crescent 59 F4
Queens Drive 63 F6
Queens Gardens 58 C3
  Victoria Crescent Road
Queens Gate Lane 58 C3
  Victoria Crescent Road
Queens Place 58 C3
Queensborough 58 A2
  Gardens
Queensferry Street 64 C6
Queenslie Street 61 H4

R
Radnor Street 58 D5
  Argyle Street
Raeberry Street 59 F3
Rafford Street 62 A1
Raglan Street 59 G4
Rathlin Street 58 A6
Ratho Drive 60 C1
Ravel Row 65 H3
Ravelston Street 65 H2
Red Road 61 F2
Red Road Court 61 F3
Redan Street 64 D3
Redford Street 61 H6
Redlands Lane 58 C2
Redlands Road 58 C2
Redlands Terrace 58 C2
  Julian Avenue
Redlands Terrace 58 C2
  Lane
Redmoss Street 59 H1
Rednock Street 60 A2
Redwood Drive 61 E3
Regent Moray 58 D5
  Street
Regent Park 63 F6
  Square
Reid Place 64 D4
Reid Street 64 D5
Reidvale Street 64 D2
Renfield Lane 63 H1
  Hope Street
Renfield Street 63 H1
Renfrew Court 59 H6
Renfrew Lane 59 H6
  Hope Street
Renfrew Street 59 H6
Renton Street 60 A5
Rhymer Street 60 C5
Rhynie Drive 62 B3

Riccarton Street 64 A6
Richard Street 63 G1
  Cadzow Street
Richmond Street 64 B1
Rimsdale Street 65 E3
Ringford Street 60 D3
Risk Street 64 C3
Ritchie Street 63 G4
Riverview Drive 63 G2
Riverview Gardens 63 G2
Riverview Place 63 G2
Robert Drive 58 A6
Robert Street 58 A6
Roberton Avenue 62 C6
Robertson Lane 63 H1
Robertson Street 63 H1
Robson Grove 63 H5
Rock Street 59 H3
Rockbank Place 65 E3
Rockbank Street 65 E3
Rockcliffe Street 64 D5
Rockfield Place 61 G1
Rockfield Road 61 G1
Rodney Street 59 H4
Roebank Street 61 F6
Rogart Street 64 D3
Rona Street 61 F4
Ropework Lane 64 A2
  Clyde Street
Rose Street 59 H5
Roseberry Street 64 C5
Rosemount 60 D6
  Crescent
Rosemount Street 60 D5
Rosevale Street 58 A4
Roslea Drive 65 E1
Rosneath Street 58 A6
Ross Street 64 B2
Rosslyn Terrace 58 C2
Rosyth Road 64 C6
Rosyth Street 64 C6
Rottenrow 60 B6
Rottenrow East 64 B1
Rowallan Gardens 58 A3
Rowallan Lane East 58 A3
Rowan Gardens 62 B4
Rowan Road 62 B4
Rowchester Street 65 E3
Roxburgh Lane 58 D3
  Saltoun Street
Roxburgh Street 58 D3
Roy Street 60 B3
Royal Bank Place 64 A1
  Buchanan Street
Royal Crescent 59 E6
Royal Exchange 64 A1
  Buildings
  Royal Exchange Square
Royal Exchange 64 A1
  Square
Royal Terrace 59 E5
Royal Terrace Lane 59 E5
Royston Road 60 C5
Royston Square 60 C5
Roystonhill 60 D5
Ruby Street 65 E4
Ruchill Place 59 F1
  Ruchill Street
Ruchill Street 59 E1
Rumford Street 64 D5
Rupert Street 59 F4
Rushyhill Street 61 E2
Ruskin Lane 59 E3
Ruskin Place 59 E3
  Great Western Road
Ruskin Terrace 59 E3
Russell Street 58 B4
  Vine Street
Rutherglen Bridge 64 D5
Rutherglen Road 64 B5
Ruthven Lane 58 D3
Ruthven Street 58 D3
Rutland Court 63 E2
  Govan Road
Rutland Crescent 63 E2

Rutland Place 63 E2
Rye Crescent 61 F1
Rye Road 61 F1
Ryebank Road 61 G1
Ryefield Road 61 F1
Ryehill Place 61 G1
Ryehill Road 61 G1
Ryemount Road 61 G1
Ryeside Road 61 F1

S
Saint Andrews 63 E4
  Crescent
Saint Andrews 63 G5
  Cross
Saint Andrews 62 D5
  Drive
Saint Andrews Lane 64 B2
  Gallowgate
Saint Andrews 63 F4
  Road
Saint Andrews 64 B2
  Square
Saint Andrews 64 B2
  Street
Saint Clair Street 59 F4
  North Woodside Road
Saint Enoch Place 63 H2
  Howard Street
Saint Enoch 64 A2
  Shopping Centre
Saint Enoch Square 63 H2
Saint Georges Place 59 G5
  Saint Georges Road
Saint Georges Road 59 G4
Saint James Road 60 B6
Saint John's Court 63 E4
Saint John's 63 E4
  Quadrant
Saint John's Road 63 E5
Saint Joseph's 60 D5
  Court
Saint Joseph's 60 D5
  Place
Saint Joseph's View 60 D5
Saint Margarets 64 A2
  Place
  Bridgegate
Saint Marnock 65 E3
  Street
Saint Marys Lane 63 H1
  West Nile Street
Saint Michael's 65 G3
  Court
  Saint Michael's Lane
Saint Michael's 65 G3
  Lane
Saint Monance 60 D1
  Street
Saint Mungo 60 A6
  Avenue
Saint Mungo Place 60 B6
Saint Ninian Terrace 64 A3
  Ballater Street
Saint Peters Lane 63 G1
  Blythswood Street
Saint Peter's Path 59 G4
  Braid Street
Saint Peters Street 59 G4
Saint Rollox Brae 60 C4
Saint Vincent 58 D6
  Crescent
Saint Vincent 58 D6
  Crescent Lane
Saint Vincent Lane 59 G6
  Hope Street
Saint Vincent Place 64 A1
Saint Vincent 59 G6
  Street
Saint Vincent 59 F6
  Terrace
Salamanca Street 65 H3
Salisbury Street 63 H4
Salkeld Street 63 H4

Salmona Street 59 H2
Saltmarket 64 A2
Saltmarket Place 64 A2
  Bridgegate
Saltoun Gardens 58 D3
  Roxburgh Street
Saltoun Lane 58 D3
Saltoun Street 58 C3
Sanda Street 59 E2
Sandfield Street 59 E1
Sandiefield Road 64 A4
Sandmill Street 61 E5
Sandringham Lane 58 D3
  Kersland Street
Sandy Lane 58 A4
  Crawford Street
Sandy Road 58 A5
Sandyfaulds Square 64 A4
Sandyfaulds Street 64 A4
Sandyford Place 59 F6
  Sauchiehall Street
Sandyford Place 59 E6
  Lane
Sandyford Street 58 C6
Sannox Gardens 61 F6
Saracen Head Lane 64 C2
  Gallowgate
Saracen Street 60 A3
Sardinia Lane 58 D3
Sardinia Terrace 58 D3
  Cecil Street
Sauchiehall Lane 59 G6
  Sauchiehall Street
Sauchiehall Street 59 G6
Savoy Street 64 D4
Sawmillfield Street 59 H4
Schipka Passage 64 B2
  Gallowgate
Scone Street 60 A3
Scotland Street 63 F3
Scotland Street 63 E3
  West
Scotsburn Road 61 G2
Scotstoun Mill Road 58 C5
  Partick Bridge Street
Scott Street 59 G6
Seagrove Street 65 H2
Seamore Street 59 F4
Seath Street 64 A6
Seaward Lane 63 E2
Seaward Place 63 E4
Seaward Street 63 F3
Second Gardens 62 A4
Seton Terrace 64 D1
Shaftesbury Street 59 F6
Shakespeare Street 59 E1
Shamrock Street 59 G5
  New City Road
Shanks Street 59 E1
Shannon Street 59 F1
Shaw Street 58 A6
Shawfield Drive 64 C6
Shawfield 64 D6
  Industrial Estate
Shawfield Road 64 D5
Shearer Street 63 F2
  Paisley Road
Shelley Court 58 A1
Sheppard Street 60 C2
  Cowlairs Road
Sherbrooke Avenue 62 C5
Sherbrooke Drive 62 C4
Sherbrooke 62 C5
  Gardens
Shettleston Road 65 H2
Shields Road 63 F3
Shipbank Lane 64 A2
  Clyde Street
Shore Street 64 D6
Shortridge Street 59 E1
Shuna Place 59 E1
Shuttle Lane 64 B1
  George Street
Shuttle Street 64 B1
Sidland Road 61 G1

Siemens Place 61 F4
Siemens Street 61 F4
Silverdale Street 65 G4
Silverfir Court 64 B5
  Silverfir Street
Silverfir Place 64 B5
Silverfir Street 64 B5
Silvergrove Street 64 C3
Simpson Street 59 F3
Skene Road 62 B3
Slatefield Court 65 E2
  Slatefield Street
Slatefield Street 65 E2
Sloy Street 60 B2
Snowdon Place 64 B4
  Benthall Street
Snowdon Street 64 B4
  Benthall Street
Society Street 65 F3
Soho Street 65 E3
Solway Street 64 D6
Somerset Place 59 F5
Somerset Place 59 F5
  Mews
Sorby Street 65 H3
Sorn Street 65 F5
South Annandale 63 H6
  Street
South Frederick 64 A1
  Street
South Portland 63 H3
  Street
South Woodside 59 F3
  Road
Southbank Street 65 H3
Southcroft Street 62 B1
Southloch Gardens 60 D3
Southloch Street 60 D3
Southmuir Place 58 D1
Southpark Avenue 58 D4
Southpark Lane 59 E4
Southpark Terrace 59 E4
  Southpark Avenue
Spiers Wharf 59 H4
Spoutmouth 64 B2
  Gallowgate
Spring Lane 64 A5
  Lawmoor Street
Springbank Street 59 F2
Springburn Road 60 C4
Springburn 60 D2
  Shopping Centre
Springburn Way 60 C2
Springfield Court 64 A1
  Buchanan Street
Springfield Quay 63 F2
Springfield Road 65 F5
Springkell Avenue 62 C5
Springkell Drive 62 B6
Springkell Gardens 62 C6
Springkell Gate 62 D6
Springvale Terrace 60 C2
Spruce Street 60 B1
Staffa Street 61 F6
Stafford Street 60 B5
Stag Street 62 B1
Stair Street 59 F2
Stamford Street 65 F3
Stanley Street 63 E3
Stanley Street Lane 63 E3
Steel Street 64 B2
Stevenson Street 64 C2
Stewart Street 59 H5
Stewartville Street 58 B4
Stirling Road 60 B6
Stirlingfauld Place 63 H3
Stobcross Road 58 D6
Stobcross Street 63 F1
Stobcross Wynd 58 C6
Stockwell Place 64 A2
Stockwell Street 64 A2
Stonyhurst Street 59 H1
Stratford Street 58 D1
Strathbran Street 65 H4
Strathclyde Street 65 E6

Striven Gardens 59 F3
Stroma Street 61 F4
Stromness Street 63 G4
Stronend Street 59 H1
Stronsay Street 61 F4
Suffolk Street 64 C2
  Kent Street
Summer Street 64 D3
Summerfield Street 65 F6
Summertown Road 62 B1
Sunnybank Street 65 F5
Sunnylaw Street 59 H2
Surrey Street 63 H4
Sussex Street 63 E3
Sutherland Avenue 62 B5
Sutherland Lane 58 C4
Swan Street 60 A5
Swanston Street 65 E6
Sword Street 64 D2
Sydenham Lane 58 B3
  Crown Road South
Sydenham Road 58 C3
Sydney Street 64 C2
Syriam Place 60 D2
  Syriam Street
Syriam Street 60 D2

T
Tamworth Street 65 E3
  Rimsdale Street
Tannock Street 59 H2
Taransay Street 58 A6
Taylor Place 60 B6
Taylor Street 64 C3
Telephone Lane 58 C3
Templeton Street 64 C3
Templetons 64 C3
  Business Centre
Terregles Avenue 62 C6
Terregles Crescent 62 B6
Terregles Drive 62 C6
Teviot Street 58 C4
Teviot Terrace 59 E2
  Sanda Street
Tharsis Street 60 D5
Third Gardens 62 A4
Thistle Terrace 64 A4
Thomson Street 65 E2
Thornbank Street 58 C5
Thornbridge 58 C1
  Avenue
  Balcarres Avenue
Thorncliffe Gardens 63 E6
Thorncliffe Lane 63 E6
Thornhill Path 65 H4
  Crail Street
Thornwood Avenue 58 A4
Thornwood 58 A4
  Gardens
Thornwood Place 58 A3
Thurso Street 58 C5
  Dunaskin Street
Tibbermore Road 58 A3
Tillie Street 59 F3
Tiree Street 61 G4

Tobago Place 64 D3
Tobago Street 64 C3
Todd Street 65 G1
Tollcross Road 65 H3
Tontine Lane 64 B2
Torness Street 58 C4
Torr Street 60 B2
Torrance Street 60 D2
Torridon Avenue 62 B5
Torridon Path 62 A5
  Dumbreck Avenue
Torrisdale Street 63 F6
Torryburn Road 61 G2
Toryglen Street 64 B6
Tower Street 63 E3
Townmill Road 60 D6
Townsend Street 60 A5
Tradeston Street 63 G3
Trafalgar Street 64 A2
Trongate 64 A2
Troon Street 65 F5
Trossachs Court 59 G3
  Trossachs Street
Trossachs Street 59 G3
Tullis Court 64 C4
Tullis Street 64 C4
Tunnel Street 63 E1
Turnberry Avenue 58 B3
  Turnberry Road
Turnberry Road 58 A3
Turnbull Street 64 B2
Turner Road 60 D4
Turnlaw Street 64 B4
Turriff Street 63 H4
Tweed Crescent 61 H5
Tyndrum Street 60 A5

U
Union Place 63 H1
  Gordon Street
Union Street 63 H1
Unity Place 59 G4
University Avenue 58 D4
University Gardens 58 D4
University of 58 D4
  Glasgow
University Place 58 D4
Urrdale Road 62 B3

V
Valleyfield Street 60 C3
  Ayr Street
Vasart Place 59 F1
Vennard Gardens 63 E6
Vermont Street 63 E3
Vicarfield Place 62 B1
  Vicarfield Street
Vicarfield Street 62 B1
Victoria Bridge 64 A2
Victoria Circus 58 C3
Victoria Crescent 58 C3
  Dowanside Road
Victoria Crescent 58 C3
  Lane

Victoria Crescent 58 C3
  Place
  Bowmont Terrace
Victoria Crescent 58 C3
  Road
Victoria Cross 63 G6
Viewfield Lane 59 E4
Viewpark Avenue 61 F6
Vine Street 58 B4
Vinicombe Lane 58 D3
Vinicombe Street 58 D3
Vintner Street 60 A4
Virginia Buildings 64 A1
  Virginia Street
Virginia Court 64 A1
  Virginia Street
Virginia Place 64 A1
Virginia Street 64 A1
Vulcan Street 60 C2
  Springburn Way

W
Waddell Court 64 B3
Waddell Street 64 B4
Walker Court 58 B5
Walker Street 58 B5
Walkinshaw Street 65 E4
Wallace Street 63 G2
Wallacewell 61 F1
  Crescent
Wallacewell Place 61 F1
Wallacewell Road 61 F1
Walls Street 64 B1
Walmer Crescent 62 C2
Walnut Crescent 60 B1
Walnut Place 60 B1
Walnut Road 60 B1
Walter Street 65 F1
Wanlock Street 58 A6
Wardhill Road 61 F1
Wardrop Street 58 A6
Warnock Street 60 C6
Warriston Crescent 61 H6
Warriston Street 61 H6
Warroch Street 63 F1
Washington Street 63 G1
Water Row 58 A6
Waterloo Lane 63 H1
  Waterloo Street
Waterloo Street 63 G1
Waterside Street 64 B4
Watson Street 64 B2
Watt Street 63 F2
Waverley Terrace 65 E2
  Whitevale Street
Weaver Street 64 B1
Webster Street 65 E5
Wellcroft Place 63 H4
Wellfield Street 60 D2
Wellington Lane 63 G1
  Blythswood Street
Wellington Street 63 H1
Wellpark Street 64 C1
West Campbell 63 G1
  Street

West End Park 59 F5
  Street
West George Lane 59 G6
  Pitt Street
West George Street 59 G6
West Graham 59 G5
  Street
West Greenhill 59 E6
  Place
West Nile Street 63 H1
West Princes Street 59 F4
West Regent Lane 59 H6
  Hope Street
West Regent Street 59 G6
West Street 63 G3
West Whitby Street 65 G4
Westbank Court 59 E4
Westbank Lane 59 E4
Westbank Quadrant 59 E4
Westbourne 58 C2
  Gardens Lane
Westbourne 58 C2
  Gardens North
Westbourne 58 C2
  Gardens South
Westbourne 58 C2
  Gardens West
Westbourne Road 58 B2
Westbourne 58 B2
  Terrace Lane
  Westbourne Road
Wester Common 59 G1
  Drive
Wester Common 59 G2
  Road
Wester Common 59 H2
  Terrace
Westercraigs 64 D1
Westercraigs Court 64 D1
  Westercraigs
Westminster 58 D3
  Gardens
  Kersland Street
Westminster 59 E6
  Terrace
  Royal Terrace
Westmoreland 63 G6
  Street
Westmuir Street 65 H3
Westside Gardens 58 B4
White Street 58 B4
Whitefield Road 62 C3
Whitehall Street 63 F1
Whitehill Gardens 65 E1
Whitehill Street 65 E1
Whitehill Street 65 E1
  Lane
Whitevale Street 65 E2
Whittingehame 58 A1
  Gardens
William Street 59 F6
Williamson Street 65 G4
Willowbank 59 F4
  Crescent
  Woodlands Road
Willowbank Street 59 F4

Wilson Street 64 A1
Wilton Crescent 59 F3
Wilton Crescent 59 F3
  Lane
Wilton Drive 59 F3
Wilton Gardens 59 F3
Wilton Street 59 E3
Windmillcroft Quay 63 G2
Windsor Street 59 G4
Windsor Terrace 59 G4
Winifred Street 61 H2
Winning Row 65 H3
Winton Drive 58 C1
Winton Lane 58 C1
Wishart Street 64 C1
Woddrop Street 65 F6
Wolseley Street 64 B5
Wood Street 61 F6
Woodhall Street 65 F6
Woodlands Drive 59 F4
Woodlands Gate 59 F4
Woodlands Road 59 F4
Woodlands Terrace 59 E5
Woodrow Circus 62 D4
Woodrow Place 62 C4
Woodrow Road 62 D4
Woodside Crescent 59 F5
Woodside Place 59 F5
Woodside Place 59 F5
  Lane
Woodside Terrace 59 F5
Woodside Terrace 59 F5
  Lane
Woodville Park 62 B2
Woodville Street 62 B2
Wyndford Drive 58 D1
Wyndford Place 58 D1
  Wyndford Road
Wyndford Road 58 D1
Wyndham Court 58 D2
  Wyndham Street
Wyndham Street 58 D2
Wyper Place 64 D2

Y
Yarrow Gardens 59 F3
Yarrow Gardens 59 F3
  Lane
Yate Street 65 F3
Yew Drive 61 E3
York Street 63 G1
Yorkhill Parade 58 C5
Yorkhill Quay 58 C6
Yorkhill Street 58 D6
Young Terrace 61 E2

Z
Zena Crescent 61 G2
Zena Place 61 H2
Zena Street 61 H2